PRAISE FOR

Appetite for Worship

Dr. Marina McLean is one of the finest Christ-centered prophetic and apostolic psalmists we know. She has been ordained by God through worship to change atmospheres, thereby ushering in the miraculous power of the Holy Spirit.

This is a must-read book for seminary professors, students, pastors, ministry leaders, choirs, and psalmists around the world. The words written ooze the creative anointing and experiential impact of over thirty years of true worship ministry!

BISHOP KEITH MCLEOD
Miracle Christian Centre International Ministries UK

Marina is one, who, by revelation, knows and reveals the biblical patterns and promises of worship that can usher believers into the manifested presence of God! Through her teaching, those who desire to know the Father and Jesus can experience the fulfillment of God's Word in the realms of glory!

PASTOR TONY KEMP
Pastor Tony Kemp Ministries, IL

To the family of God, the body of Christ, Israel, in Yeshua's name. It's an honor to express my appreciation to our Redeemer for nourishing and empowering us with the gift, Prophetess Marina McLean. I am privileged to know her as a dear friend, covenant partner, and co-laborer in God's kingdom. She brings God's glory, His presence, and His power in a manner that surpasses human intellect. Her worship, revelatory insight, and wisdom for bringing His glorious presence in conferences and churches to all ethnic groups is phenomenal. Prophetess Marina is very gracious and passionate about the body experiencing God and the miraculous, deeper dimensions of His heart. She carries the sound of the nations, and God has truly given her a grace to bring heaven to earth.

For those who endeavor to witness a greater glory with clear understanding of revelation, what you are about to receive will bring you the answers to questions in your heart. You are about to be enlightened! This is not just a writing, but a divine moment to build your future with confidence. May heaven saturate your conscience as you head into eternity with Marina McLean.

APOSTLE JEROME A. PARKER, Ohio

Appetite for Worship

Appetite for Worship

Creating a Hunger
for His Presence

Marina McLean

CREATIVE ENTERPRISES STUDIO

BEDFORD, TEXAS

Appetite for Worship

Copyright © 2017 Marina McLean.

All rights reserved. No portion of this book may be reproduced, stored in a retrieval system, or transmitted in any form or by any means—electronic, mechanical, photocopy, recording, scanning, or other—except for brief quotations in critical reviews or articles, or as specifically allowed by the U. S. Copyright Act of 1976, as amended, without the prior written permission of the publisher.

Published in association with Books, Bach & Beyond, Inc. d/b/a Creative Enterprises Studio, 1507 Shirley Way, Bedford, TX 76022. CreativeEnterprisesStudio.com.

Cover Design: Dugan Design Group
Interior Image: www.istockphoto.com
Interior Design: Inside-Out Design & Typesetting, Hurst, TX

Unless otherwise noted, Scripture quotations are from the Anglican King James Version. Public domain.

Scripture quotations designated NIV are taken from the Holy Bible, New International Version®, NIV®. Copyright © 1973, 1978, 1984, 2011 by International Bible Society. Used by permission of Zondervan Bible Publishers.

ISBN: 978-0-9911889-7-0 Softcover

978-0-9911889-8-7 e-Book

Library of Congress Control Number: 2017941449

Printed in the United States of America

17 18 19 20 21 22   MG   6 5 4 3 2 1

Dedication

To my late parents –

Pastor Charles Headlam for his endless training in how to deal with a determined man who loved quietly and fondly. Dad loved quoting the Proverbs as his mode of discipline to me. I didn't know they were Bible scriptures until I learned to look them up. I always thought they were Caribbean parables.

Clarice Headlam for her strength, wisdom, compassion, and her gift of reading a room. I miss her voice and the practical jokes I loved playing on her and my dad. I began my spiritual hunger accompanying Mom to conferences; then, as I began to travel, she became my companion and armor bearer.

My mom was alive when I started writing this book, and she helped me choose the book cover.

Mom and Dad, your legacy of faith will continue throughout my generation.

To my younger sister, Cheryl, for encouraging me to mentor her and being the inspiration for my strength.

Contents

	Foreword	xi
	Acknowledgments	xiii
	Introduction	xv
1	The Origin of Worship	1
2	Heaven's Vocabulary	5
3	The Prophets' Response	11
4	The Angels' Response	15
5	The Response of the Redeemed	25
6	Faith Is in the Sound Dimension of God	33
7	Distinct Sounds	37
8	Corporate Worship	45
9	Acts of Praise	53

Contents

10	Expression of Worship	59
11	Personal Revelation	65
12	Supernatural Worship	71
13	Prophetic Worship	77
14	Living Sacrifice	85
15	My Testimony	93
	My Worship Journal	99
	Glossary	103
	About the Author	105

Foreword

When I was a young boy, I remember the beginning of each church service was known as the song service, and it was usually an exuberant time when believers would sing the words from what was referred to as a song book. Basically, the songs were poetry put to music.

Song writing was done mainly by those whom the church world depended upon to furnish new songs, and occasionally, there would be fresh anthems for everyone to learn. In my lifetime, I have witnessed those song services being transformed into something marvelous I never could have imagined.

It is evident that during the Charismatic Renewal, as the Holy Spirit guided the body of Christ into revelation regarding divine healing and the fullness of the Spirit, as well as prophetic phenomena and presence-based ministries, worship played a vital role in that journey.

The transformation of worship has been amazing to witness: it has gone from inspiration to revelation in just a few decades. Worship morphed from just singing songs into seeding atmospheres. In Psalm 102:18, David, the great psalmist, spoke of a future generation of worshippers. Think of it, a generation of people created to praise the Lord! God's way is to move from better to best and from glory to greater glory. You can be assured that the Holy Spirit will move the sounds of the church from crescendo to greater crescendo before our

Foreword

Lord's presence.

My friend, Marina McLean, has penned a revelatory treatise. Her new book, *Appetite for Worship*, offers much-needed insight into what may lie ahead in the glorious realm of worship. As I began reading this book, I was thrilled to find a rare combination of clear commitment to the Word of God and clear insight about where worship may be headed. This book is not only academic, but every chapter is filled with revelatory patterns. I believe Marina has published this book at this *kairos* to help equip this generation of worshippers to assemble in song before the Lord.

John Kilpatrick
Founder, In His Presence Church; Daphne, AL

Acknowledgments

My very special thanks . . .

To my husband, Renny, for the thirty-five years he has inspired me "to go higher" when I lead worship. The revelation that flows out of his spirit challenges, corrects, instructs, inspires me; it demands my attention and awakens my imagination. These key responses encourage the worship that flows out of me. As he ascends to the heavens, I am provoked to jealousy, wanting my expression of the heavenly realms to match those that exude from his revelation.

To my three young adult children, Maranatha, Caleb, and Zoe, who teach me every day through their discipline and dedication to detail in their spheres of influence to excel using technology.

To my parents, the late Clarice and the late Charles Headlam. Music was always alive in my home. Mom sang alto in the church choir, and Dad was a bass in the adult choir and quartet. Both gave me a legacy of faith and believing God for the impossible things. Dad nurtured in me a love for the Old Testament, and Mom fostered my passion for the supernatural. Mom and I were considered rebels when we started going to the Morris Cerullo crusades in London when I was nine years old. This book will always be special to me, because

Acknowledgments

my mom helped me choose the cover. I know they are both watching and cheering me on from the cloud of witnesses that accompany me on this Christian journey.

To my parents-in-law, Mavis and George McLean, who embrace me as one of their own children. I can't tell you the number of times Mother Mac and I have had our own worship service at home with the *Redemptional Hymnal* or her favorite choruses.

To my spiritual parents, Mama Billie and Papa Al, for encouraging me to be an ascending woman in the presence of God. Their love and prayer support impacts how I begin a worship service at our conferences.

To all my spiritual children, both here in the United States and around the world, who have watched me grow in the Lord and encouraged me to touch heaven to change their atmosphere on earth.

To the staff at Renny McLean Ministries, who have kept me disciplined and held me to deadlines: Jay Rischer and Wanda White, thank you.

To Mary Hollingsworth and the Creative Enterprises Studio team, who took the time to grasp the vision and interpret my heart, thank you.

Introduction

I want to welcome you to *Appetite for Worship*, where I hope you will experience what it is to be a worshipper. I hope this journey will take you from the outer courts, through the inner courts into the Holy of Holies, hearing the voice of God, knowing His presence, and then responding to His presence.

The journey I take you on is my life as a worshipper. I have learned how to worship God with hymns, songs, and spiritual songs. I desire for you to become a spontaneous worshipper, where you know your voice matters, and the song in your heart is received. Wherever you are, you can make a joyful noise unto the Lord and create an atmosphere for Him to come and respond to you.

I want to encourage you to develop the ability to respond to the voice of God the first time He speaks to your inner man. As a worshipper, your relationship with the Lord is very important. I pray you will open your heart, your spirit, your mind, and your strength to this journey of worship and intimacy with the Lord your God and Creator of all things.

Introduction

> Wherever you are, you can make a joyful noise unto the Lord and create an atmosphere for Him to come and respond to you.

Join me on this journey into the *Appetite for Worship* and learn more about the One you worship and who you are as a worshipper.

1
The Origin of Worship

The origin of worship is heaven. It began when God created the angels and all their ranks. However, we don't discover this in Genesis 1, at the creation of the world; we discover it in Revelation 4 when John was transported into the heavens and given a worship experience that will change his hunger for the presence of God, and whet our own appetite for that heavenly worship.

Worship began with God wanting it in the heavens. He created the angels to worship Him, and the sound dimension was birthed with a heavenly sound from the angels responding to the presence and works of God. While God provides us with a picture of worship in Genesis 1, where He records how the earth was created, with all the facets and details, the heavens remain a mystery to us. This mystery doesn't unfold until we read Revelation 4. We will be looking at these scriptures in more depth throughout the book.

Though the origin of worship is in heaven, it was perfected on earth. The sound dimension of worship, the singing of a chorus, the responding back and forth from the angels all began in heaven. However, the full expression of that worship could be put into an extensive vocabulary and posture when God created man in His image and likeness. We will be exploring this further in the upcoming chapters, but for now I want to whet your appetite for worship.

The word for worship in Hebrew is *sagad*, meaning to prostrate, bow down, or posture. The Greek word for worship is *proskuneo*, meaning to bend or to lay flat before Him. Notice that both words denote posture.

God wants you to bring your posture, your expression, into worship. The Hebrew word implies that worship is about intimacy—about your intimate relationship with God, which is one of the aspects I love about worship. Intimacy draws you to God. It suggests that you must abandon who you are, what you think, and how you think it. Intimacy implies closeness or familiarity. When you come before God and there is an exchange of secrets and mysteries, you want God's thoughts, not your thoughts. And thus it becomes a wonderful relationship that begins with the heart of a worshipper knowing God.

There are innumerable aspects of worship in its original state. We see it in its original creativity in the heavens. However, we only learn about worship in the heavens through John after his relationship with Jesus. John was sent in exile to the Isle of Patmos, and in a place of despair, he encountered God in a very real way. No man had this full experience with the vocabulary to explain heaven's worship service as John did; only the Holy Spirit could provide the words through him.

Jesus opened the door or became the entrance for John to go into heaven to witness this worship experience or revelation. John represented a different generation who would speak to a generation to come who would be able to understand and respond with worship and knowledge far beyond John's day—a different vocabulary, imagination, technology, and understanding.

In Revelation 4:1–11 he recorded:

> After this I looked, and, behold, a door was opened in heaven, and the first voice which I heard was as it were of a trumpet talking with me; which said, Come up hither and I will shew

The Origin of Worship

thee things which must be hereafter. And immediately I was in the spirit: and, behold, a throne was set in heaven and one sat on the throne, and he that sat was to look upon like a jasper and a sardine stone: and there was a rainbow round about the throne, in sight like unto an emerald. And round about the throne were four and twenty seats: and upon the seats I saw four and twenty elders sitting, clothed in white raiment; and they had on their heads crowns of gold. And out of the throne proceeded lightnings and thunderings and voices: and there were seven lamps of fire burning before the throne, which are the seven Spirits of God. And before the throne there was a sea of glass like unto crystal: and in the midst of the throne, and round about the throne, were four beasts full of eyes before and behind. And the first beast was like a lion, and the second beast like a calf, and the third beast had a face as a man, and the fourth beast was like a flying eagle. And the four beasts had each of them six wings about him; and they were full of eyes within: and they rest not day and night, saying, Holy, holy, holy, Lord God Almighty, which was, and is, and is to come. And when those beasts give glory and honor and thanks to him that sat on the throne, who liveth for ever and ever, the four and twenty elders fall down before him that sat on the throne, and worship him that liveth for ever and ever, and cast their crowns before the throne, saying, Thou art worthy, O Lord, to receive glory and honor and power: for thou has created all things and for thy pleasure they are and were created.

When you read those verses, you get a revelation, an understanding, an unveiling of what worship is like in the heavens, and what it's been like from the foundation of the earth until now. The creation is surrounding the throne, singing, "Holy, holy, holy," and they are still witnessing things they simply cannot express.

Everything in heaven is continually responding. The four beasts have their own form of expression; the elders remove their crowns and throw them before the Lord. As with the elders, whatever position, whatever authority, whatever role I play, when I stand in worship, I abandon who I am and what I'm about because I'm caught up in the moment with God.

When you read those verses, you get a revelation, an understanding, an unveiling of what worship is like in the heavens, and what it's been like from the foundation of the earth until now.

Yes, the origin of worship was in the heavens, and we are given this picture of everyone working in harmony, everyone knowing his or her role, knowing the part he or she plays. But it's also interesting to note that each one had a specific response. The angels surrounding the throne, the four beasts with outstretched wings—the only vocabulary they have is "Holy, holy, holy," which had been said long before God said, "Let there be light," and separated the heavens from the earth (Gen. 1).

2
Heaven's Vocabulary

The angels' vocabulary is "holy, holy, holy."

From the creation of the heavens, before the earth and the universe were made, in what is called eternity past, the angels were given a timeless expression that would go beyond any language barrier to come.

Why do we call it eternity past? Worship was happening before the earth was created, and we are told in the book of Revelation that the Lamb was slain before the foundations of the earth: "And all that dwell upon the earth shall worship him, whose names are not written in the book of life of the Lamb slain from the foundation of the world" (13:8).

Every creation of God knows how to say "holy." The description of the beasts represents the faces of mankind and the domination, or territorial authority, of each creature made by God. The lion dominates the animal kingdom; God would require the calf as a sacrifice; the face of a man represents the God-ordained ruler of all created things; and the eagle dominates the fowl of the air.

The description of these creatures includes wings that continue in movement day and night. We are also told they have eyes in their wings, eyes in front, eyes behind, which represent the all-seeing eyes of God. However, they also represent all the time zones. There are no time constraints in heaven; there is no past, present, or future. Everything is one continuum of time called the now!

Therefore, these creatures are seeing all the things God is doing on the earth continually, and their response, or vocabulary, is "Holy, holy, holy." God always speaks two or three times to establish a point, or to confirm that something is really from Him. We say, to repeat is to reinforce.

THE ELDERS' VOCABULARY

The elders have slightly more expression and vocabulary than the creatures surrounding the throne. The elders have a more human appearance and apparel. They also represent the leadership or governments of the earth. There are twenty-four elders in heaven, and they represent the governmental number of the heavens, since the number twelve usually represents governments. In Hebrew twelve is the number of authority and perfection. Exodus 28:21 says, "And the stones shall be with the names of the children of Israel, twelve, according to their names, like the engravings of a signet; every one with his name shall they be according to the twelve tribes." Having twenty-four elders illustrates that heaven's governments are higher than earth's.

> The twenty-four elders declare the Lord is worthy to receive glory and honor, and they acknowledge that all things were created for His good pleasure.

Heaven's Vocabulary

The twenty-four elders declare the Lord is worthy to receive glory and honor, and they acknowledge that all things were created for His good pleasure. Their witness to the creation of God's works produces a deeper response, and the elders go beyond words by removing their crowns and throwing them at the foot of the throne of God. Sometimes there is simply no vocabulary for what we witness the hand of God display. Our language is insufficient, so our expression yields the highest language of worship before God. There comes a time when the bowing down and laying at the throne all that we worked for, reveals the glory that comes from the victories and battles fought. The elders laid down the crowns that were evidence of their titles, victories, riches, and honor.

That is one of the greatest challenges in our worship today: as God gives us increase in the kingdom, can we still bow low and bring Him an expression that shows we honor Him beyond the evidence of things? My friend, that is why our expression and posture in worship are so important. The more battles we win, the more we overcome, the more titles or honor we receive, the more we must give God an expression that speaks as loudly as our vocal worship.

THE HOST OF ANGELS AND THEIR RESPONSE TO ONE ANOTHER

John told us this in Revelation 5:8–14:

> And when he had taken the book, the four beasts and four and twenty elders fell down before the Lamb, having every one of them harps, and golden vials full of odors, which are the prayers of saints. And they sung a new song, saying, Thou art worthy to take the book, and to open the seals thereof: for thou wast slain, and hast redeemed us to God by thy blood out of every kindred, and tongue, and people, and nation; And hast made us unto our God kings and priests: and we shall reign on the earth. And I beheld, and I heard the voice of many

angels round about the throne and the beasts and the elders: and the number of them was ten thousand times ten thousand, and thousands of thousands, saying with a loud voice, Worthy is the Lamb that was slain to receive power, and riches, and wisdom, and strength, and honor, and glory, and blessing. And every creature which is in heaven, and on the earth, and under the earth, and such as are in the sea, and all that are in them, heard I saying, Blessing, and honor, and glory, and power, be unto him that sitteth upon the throne, and unto the Lamb for ever and ever. And the four beasts said, Amen. And the four and twenty elders fell down and worshipped him that liveth for ever and ever.

This is the worship experience I look forward to having when I enter a prayer meeting or when I'm in the heights of worship. It is the kind of worship that takes place when breakthroughs are happening, as we petition heaven for revelation, intercession, and miracles. The angels carry our vases and bring them before the host of angels, who respond to our petitions. We get a picture that our prayers are stored in vases or vials the angels watch over until our prayers are fulfilled on the earth. There becomes a knowing we cannot explain, but we have faith that God watches over the petitions of our hearts, and the angels are described as ministering servants who work on our behalf to bring the evidence of our overdue prayers. Psalms 91:11 says, "For he shall give his angels charge over thee, to keep thee in all thy ways." Then they have a different response. Their song is transformed by new levels of intercession, because in heaven the Holy Spirit's influence requires a new song. We may believe we desire to join in with the angels, but I challenge you that the angels want to join in with us.

When I imagine the angels with the vases of our prayers, the picture speaks to me of accumulation. The breakthrough is in the collecting of prayers, the collection of faith. This evidence of a breakthrough demands or requires a reply from a rank of angels who will sing in response to our requests or petitioning heaven on behalf of earth. Glory brings a movement the heavens have not yet seen—an unwitnessed display of God—and the angels have to sing a new song to keep in rhythm with us.

Can you imagine that heaven is responding continuously to the victories happening all over the earth with the children of God? Their response is to sing a *new* song, and not use the vocabulary that has been assigned to them since the beginning of time.

3
The Prophets' Response

Listen to Isaiah the prophet continue his marvelous description of the Lord in His temple:

> In the year that king Uzziah died I saw also the Lord sitting upon a throne, high and lifted up, and his train filled the temple. Above it stood the seraphim: each one had six wings; with two he covered his face, and with two he covered his feet, and with two he did fly. And one cried unto another, and said Holy, holy, holy, is the LORD of hosts: the whole earth is full of his glory. (6:1–3)

This passage in Isaiah is the first recording in the Old Testament of worship that matches the description as worship before the foundations of the earth. It mirrors what we read in Revelation, establishing that worship has no time constraints and is a continual rhythm and movement of God.

God's sound was established before the foundations of the earth, and it has not changed. He desires to interact with us in the realm of worship. I love this visual of interaction God gave me years ago, and it has changed the way I worship and write songs. Everything must respond to the presence of God. As He is moving, we are responding to Him. God speaks and the earth responds; the earth petitions God, and the heavens respond with God.

Isaiah 6:4 continues with another visual of the earth's response to God: "And the posts of the door moved at the voice of him that cried, and the house was filled with smoke."

The doorposts do not have a voice, yet they responded to the presence of God and all His glory. This tells us everything that is created, whether by man or by God, knows the presence of God and longs to be a part of the expression of worship that we bring to the Lord our God.

Let's take a little detour for a moment and explore the account where Jesus was riding into Jerusalem, and the religious leaders of the day were angry at the response of the crowd. They admonished Jesus to silence the spontaneous worship service, which had broken the worship traditions of their day. What was Jesus's response? "And he answered and said unto them, I tell you that, if these should hold their peace, the stones would immediately cry out" (Luke 19:40).

What a shock to the leaders of that day. They could not recognize or acknowledge the Christ, but even more absurd for them, the rocks beneath them, which they held in no regard, could recognize and wanted to be a part of the celebration. Isaiah proclaimed, "The trees of the field shall clap their hands" (55:12).

All of creation knows how to respond to God, and yet man can stand in the presence of our Lord and still debate and reason why He should not be worshipped.

The Prophets' Response

All of creation knows how to respond to God, and yet man can stand in the presence of our Lord and still debate and reason why He should not be worshipped. This is an injustice to our God.

I love to imagine that when we stand in the presence of God, experiencing His presence in a way for which we have no reference, it demands something new from us. Can you imagine, this doorpost had heard worship and sacrifice ascending to the Lord from its inception, but this was the first time the presence of God had shown up in this fashion, causing the doorpost to be a part of the worship service too? The psalmist sings, "Let every thing that hath breath praise the Lord" (Ps. 150:6). I would like to add, let everything that has been created respond to the present glory of God in the atmosphere and moment.

All creation has an expression or a posture in the presence of our God. Throughout my worship experience, I have noticed everyone has their own posture in the presence of God. There is no uniform method. People will cry, stand still, bow their heads, stretch out their arms, lie flat on their faces or on their backs, put their hands over their faces, and show serious faces, and some just smile. None of these expressions is wrong; they are the individuals' unique responses.

EZEKIEL'S DESCRIPTION

And I looked, and, behold, a whirlwind came out of the north, a great cloud, and a fire enfolding itself, and a brightness was about it, and out of the midst thereof as the color of amber, out of the midst of the fire. Also out of the midst thereof came the likeness of four living creatures. And this was their appearance; they had the likeness of a man. And every one had four faces, and every one had four wings. And their feet were straight feet; and the sole of their feet was like the sole of a calf's foot: and they sparkled like the color of burnished brass. And they had the hands of a man under their wings on their four sides; and they four had their faces and their wings. Their wings were joined one to another; they turned not when they went; they went every one straight forward. (Ezek. 1:4–9)

Ezekiel gives us a deeper description of the creatures around the throne, and he is the first one to give us the description in color—amber burnished brass. In Scripture, brass represents judgment. This color testified to the ministry relationship that Ezekiel would have with the children of Israel. God demonstrated through Ezekiel the event that would unfold against Israel as the judgment of God.

In this description of worship, we see the unison of movement in their response to the presence of God. This is the first time we are given the description of color and choreography of worship. In this case, Ezekiel was only an observer; he was not permitted to be a part of it.

I want you to understand the significance of the creatures and what they represent to us. They have the understanding of a man and far more. The lion exhibits strength, fierceness, and boldness. An ox represents diligence, patience, and unwearied perseverance in the work it must do. An eagle excels in quickness, piercing sight, and in soaring high. And finally, the angels excel man in all these respects. Each also represents the dominion it has in its individual kingdom. In everything God created there is an expression in man that demonstrates dominion and creativity in our responses to God.

4
The Angels' Response

At the birth of Jesus, the angels gave their witness in song:

> And this shall be a sign unto you; Ye shall find the babe wrapped in swaddling clothes, lying in a manger. And suddenly there was with the angel a multitude of the heavenly host praising God, and saying, Glory to God in the highest, and on earth peace, good will toward men. (Luke 2:12–14)

Do you get the impression the angels were not content to be part of the observation team, nor content simply to announce the birth of the Messiah? They wanted to lead the worship on earth. They wanted to give their witness or testimony on earth. The angelic host left their witness in song to be recorded forever. This is the first worship experience of angels in the New Testament, and they are again acknowledging the mighty acts of God.

The angels had been praising God in the heavens since eternity, but this is the first time their voiceprint is recorded on the earth as a witness of God in the flesh. The heavenly host are worshipping deity on earth. Wow! I get chills thinking about the angels being the first to demonstrate how to worship God in the flesh on earth, offering earth an example of how to worship the King of glory!

> The angels' announcement was immediately followed by worship, synchronizing heaven and earth in one worship experience.

Up until this time the prophets only prophesied about the Messiah. They did not supply any protocol of how to worship Immanuel, "God with us," or envision the future with the Holy Spirit indwelling us and teaching us another form of expression in worship.

The angels' announcement was immediately followed by worship, synchronizing heaven and earth in one worship experience. I love that the Bible records this heavenly host worshipping, giving the example again that heaven responds to what is taking place on earth.

As we are discussing the ranks of angels and their expression, there is one example of angels being seen, but only the voice of God is heard. In Genesis, God visits Jacob, giving him access to the heavens. This is the only time a ladder is mentioned in the Bible.

Jacob was preparing to see his brother, Esau, years after he stole Esau's birthright, and Jacob was afraid. God visited him to establish again the covenant of the blessing he had stolen.

> And he dreamed, and behold a ladder set up on the earth, and the top of it reached to heaven: and behold the angels of God ascending and descending on it. And, behold, the Lord stood above it, and said, I am the Lord God of Abraham thy father, and the God of Isaac: the land whereon thou liest, to thee will I give it, and to thy seed. (Gen. 28:12–13)

The Angels' Response

The first thing God used to establish access to the heavens was His voice. Second, Jacob's ability to see the ladder gave him access into the heavens. God allowed Jacob to witness the angels' testimony in the heavens as they surrounded the ladder, but Jacob didn't hear the angels' song; he heard only the voice of God.

Again, we hear and see God introducing Himself and reminding Jacob of the covenant He had made with his father and grandfather. Our God will always give us evidence for worshipping Him and believing Him for greater things. Please note that Jacob was having this experience while he was afraid and in torment. He had evidence—the blessings—of the stolen birthright, but he was going to meet his past (his brother, Esau) with the fruits of those blessings. Jacob had been blessed by God under the birthright of his brother. He had evidence and character to keep pursing the birthright. However, during this wrestling with God, God called Jacob by his covenant name, Israel, and established the blessing and legacy in his name.

Our identities are established when we encounter God. Every new season of our lives demands a new altar, new consecration, a reinforcing of our identities and purpose from God. When you have struggled with who you are, and you finally have been assigned a purpose, an encounter where God calls you as He has always seen you is a life-changing moment. To everyone who knew him, Jacob meant "mischievous, crafty in nature, deceiver." Under this name, Jacob had to struggle with his father-in-law, Laban, but because of destiny and purpose, Jacob was still blessed. He left Laban's house with the evidence of his birthright, and God changed Jacob's name to Israel, meaning in Hebrew "triumphant with God." I would like to emphasize here the importance of an encounter with God so that our identities can be established for the purpose of being a blessing to those we are called to serve. God's eternal covenant will always give us a reminder to worship Him when doubt and discouragement set in. My prayer for you:

Appetite for Worship

Lord, give us access to the heavens, the revelation of the heavens, the sounds of the heavens, the vocabulary of the heavens, and the boldness to always come before You even with a broken spirit. Let courage envelope us like a blanket and keep us strong in all that You are asking us to do.

THE HEAVENLY VOCABULARY

We have glimpsed the angels who respond to what they see by saying "Holy," and then we've witnessed another set of angels, a different rank, who declare what they see. Each rank has their special expression. The image I have of the heavens is that each section is responding or answering the other. A version of this is often done in the congregation in four sections, with each section taking a line and responding back and forth. With the assistance of musicians, I have put this four-part call and response to melody.

1. Worthy is the Lamb that was slain to receive power,
2. Riches, wisdom, strength, honor, glory, and blessing;
3. Blessing, honor, glory, and power;
4. Unto Him that sits on the throne, [all together] and unto the Lamb forever and ever.

I hope this creates a visual image for you! I have done this demonstration in a few of my worship workshops and it is powerful. It is a joy to see the audience responding back and forth with the vocabulary of the angels, and then to see the twenty-four elders bowing down because they have no more words. We get a glimpse of heaven's response on earth, and yet there is no vocabulary of the new song without us.

Revelation 5:9 records the one time in Scripture when the angels' song changed: "And they sang a new song, saying, Thou art worthy to take the book, and to open the seals thereof: for thou wast slain, and hast redeemed us to God by thy blood out of every kindred, and tongue, and people, and nation."

The angels could only sing this new song when they had the prayers of the saints. They were responding to and worshipping with the weeping saints, who were believing God for things they had not yet experienced and for breakthroughs into the unknown. They sang our songs with us in the realms of the heavens.

Worship started in the heavens, and as awesome as it was, something was missing.

It's important to understand we're trying to be a part of worship in the heavens, and one thing I've learned is that worship in the heavens is a response to the worship and activity on earth. Also worship on earth is a response to worship in the heavens. This creates a continual cycle of synchronicity in worship going up to the Lord. Keep in mind, I'm not talking about praise; I'm talking about worship.

The angels understand who God is. They understand the works of God, yet they don't know and have never received that redemptive power from the blood of Jesus.

The angels understand who God is. They understand the works of God, yet they don't know and have never received that redemptive power from the blood of Jesus. Therefore their worship is completely different from ours because we've been redeemed by the blood of the Lamb, and we were made in His likeness and in His image. Does that impact and excite you? O, hallelujah! It excites me!

THE ANGELS' REVELATION

In Revelation 11:17 we are told that the angels' revelation of God in the heavens is God Almighty: "We give thee thanks, O Lord God Almighty, which art, and wast, and art to come; because thou hast taken to thee thy great power, and hast reigned."

> The angels did not only worship God because of His mighty acts on the earth; they worshipped God because they had a revelation of who He is.

The angels did not only worship God because of His mighty acts on the earth; they worshipped God because they had a revelation of who He is. The worship in heaven is a corporate environment, and yet God had a plan reserved that would take worship to another level of response.

Why? Because God made something different when He made man in His image and likeness. The Bible mentions three angels by name, two of whom we talk about more than the other: Gabriel and Michael. But Scripture also names Lucifer—Satan—in his original name and state.

The first time we read about Gabriel is in the book of Daniel: "And I heard a man's voice between the banks of Ulai, which called, and said, Gabriel, make this man to understand the vision" (8:16). Gabriel was a special messenger sent by God to bring revelation and special instructions, often to prophets. He came to bring glad tidings beyond the prophets' understanding. When Gabriel announced himself, he lets the prophets know he was the angel that stands in the presence of God. He was not one of the worshipping angels, but a special messenger.

The Angels' Response

Our first introduction to Michael is also in the book of Daniel: "But the prince of the kingdom of Persia withstood me one and twenty days: but, lo, Michael, one of the chief princes, came to help me; and I remained there with the kings of Persia" (10:13). Michael was the warfaring angel sent to assist people when they were battling spiritual wickedness (forces we cannot explain) in high places. This passage reminds us we need heavenly artillery when we are facing territorial strongholds in the spiritual realm. It's remarkable that Daniel did not see Michael as an angel, but a prince, and Michael confirmed that he was a prince sent to strengthen him and give him instructions on how to fight this spiritual authority that is engaged in war against the nation of Israel. However, he revealed he was no ordinary prince when he asked Daniel, "Knowest thou wherefore I come unto thee? and now will I return to fight with the prince of Persia: and when I am gone forth, lo, the prince of Grecia shall come" (10:20). The prince of Persia is another reference in Hebrew to Satan, and Daniel did not have the authority, strength, revelation, and strategy to fight this battle.

When we consider the three angelic names given in Scripture—Gabriel, Michael, and Lucifer—the one we encounter the most is Lucifer. In Hebrew his original name was *heyel*, meaning "light bearer," but after his rebellion he was given the Latin name *Lucifer*.

In the book of Ezekiel, we are given a rare description of Lucifer:

> Thou hast been in Eden the garden of God; every precious stone was thy covering, the sardius, topaz, and the diamond, the beryl, the onyx, and the jasper, the sapphire, the emerald, and the carbuncle, and gold: the workmanship of thy tabrets and of thy pipes was prepared in thee in the day that thou wast created. (28:13)

This passage describes the astounding beauty of Lucifer, the priceless possessions of stones inside of him, and the sound dimension he carried. He was both the worship leader and the instrument of worship. He possessed the sounds of musical instruments before they were invented on the earth. I'm reminded of the Hammond B organ, which makes me imagine the sound of heaven before worship with instruments began on the earth. Nearly every cathedral or historic church houses these magnificent pipes for their grand sound the organs creates. However, it's imperative to understand that Lucifer carried the sound dimension of God, along with the precious stones, but he never had the song of the Lord. God reserved the vocabulary of expression for the different ranks of angels.

When we examine these three prominent messengers of God, we see the signature of God, and Lucifer's ancient Hebrew name, *heyel*, is no longer used. Rather, he is henceforth referred to as his common name, Lucifer. Notice the abbreviated Hebrew name for God is *El*; it is God's signature. "El" remains a part of *Michael* and *Gabriel*, but it is no longer found in *Lucifer*.

The sound dimension was in Lucifer, and he carried the sound of worship God loved to hear. I can imagine that as Lucifer made a sound, the different instruments' rhythm was in him. He didn't play the instruments; they were his expression as he responded to the presence of God. Lucifer's original name meant "bright star," so we can imagine he was the first light and sound in the morning to start the worship unto our God. However, once rebellion and jealousy were found in him, he could no longer bring the sound God loved to hear, so he was thrown out of heaven and banished from the presence of God.

God always knows what our outcome will be, and so He made provision for His sound and worship to be in the voiceprint of man, and not in manmade instruments. When He created Adam, He instituted worship as a relationship lifestyle that does not need anything mechanical to enhance it. The original sound of worship is in the voiceprint of man as is the ability to respond spontaneously to God.

Interestingly, in our churches today, leaders are often looking for a particular sound that reflects the word in their mouths and the sound that will become resident in their houses of worship. I challenge wor-

The Angels' Response

ship leaders to write songs from the message of their man or woman of God so the house has a dominant sound. Every worship leader is given the task to find songs for that season or songs relevant to their message. However, what we worship leaders don't take into consideration is that we are looking for a particular sound, one we can't explain or describe. We can only relate that the songs others have chosen are not the songs in our spirits.

When Lucifer wanted the worship to be all about him, he was no longer playing the sound God loved to hear. I can imagine that the sound Lucifer was now releasing was a sound the angels could not respond to, because it was not about God. The angels that were caught up in the beauty and light of Lucifer rebelled with him, but those who had their revelation of God could not follow the sound that did not mirror the atmosphere and environment of heaven.

In the early hours of the morning when God wakes us up, worship starts inside us. King David caught that revelation when he said, "Awake up, my glory; awake, psaltery and harp: I myself will awake early" (Ps. 57:8).

God did not depend on Lucifer to bring the morning sound because He knew there would be a people or nation who would worship Him. There would come a generation, multitudes who would know how to worship Him because they had God's signature, God's breath, and God's life inside them.

We know worship was created in the heavens. When we look at the story of Jesus's birth, we see the angels engaging in worship. Matthew tells us after Mary gave birth, there were shepherds in the field whose attention suddenly was drawn to the heavens because of a host of angels singing. These angels were singing a song the shepherds had never heard; there had been no such song sung on earth. The angels wanted to join in earth's response to the Christ being born. They knew Him from the heavens as the Lamb, but now they were seeing Him born on earth in human form. "And suddenly there was with the angel a multitude of the heavenly host praising God" (Luke 2:13).

The angels wanted to join in, to be a part of that celebration, and so they sang before the shepherds. As a worshipper, I can just imagine that worship service! First, I would be wondering in awe what's happening, and then I'd be drawn into the angels' worship, desiring to worship in the same way. Oh, to experience that revelation.

Again, earth has no reference from the Old Testament about how to worship Immanuel, deity in the flesh. In this moment the angels led the charge as they announced Jesus' birth and worshipped Him.

5
The Response of the Redeemed

Let's explore the times when angels joined in with what they saw happening on earth. Let's return to Revelation 4:6, where the angels and the beasts are gathered around the throne. My husband, Renny, and I love the picture painted there of the eyes in and under the angels' wings, the eyes in front of and behind them. Why? Because in the heavens there is no time—no past, present, and future. There is no compression of time, no marrying of time; everything is happening in the now.

These angels and creatures surround the throne, seeing everything. Can you visualize this? They see every century, every act being played out, every display of God being manifested. And every time they see it, they're praising God ahead of time with their eyes in front; they're praising God in the midst of time as their eyes see the present; and they're praising God for what's taken place as their eyes see earth's past.

As these angels and creatures see the whole time span of earth, they respond with us. O, hallelujah! And the more God displays Himself, the only language that they know is "Holy, holy, holy." The elders witness things that eyes have not seen and ears have not heard, and neither do the angels have an understanding of these things. "But as it is written, Eye hath not seen, nor ear heard, neither have entered into the heart of man, the things which God hath prepared for them that love him" (1 Cor. 2:9).

And so, the elders' response is to take off their crowns and throw them before the throne of God as their expression. Entering His presence, they bow down and worship.

Even with the little expression they have, they worship, but we have an unlimited amount of expression. Why? Because we've been redeemed. We were made in God's image and after His likeness. We have a testimony that speaks to the redemptive power of Jesus.

In this passage of Scripture in Revelation 5, they are singing a new song because the seals are about to be opened! There is unusual activity taking place in the heavens that demands a new sound! They have seen the Lamb slain from the foundations of the earth, and you can imagine that required a song. They have also seen the blood of the Lamb placed on the mercy seat each year according to God's timetable of atonement for the nation of Israel. And because they have a new song, a new response is reequired.

Yet, with everything the angels see and respond to with worship, they have not been dipped in the blood of the Lamb; they have not been redeemed; they have not experienced firsthand the victory of God on their behalf. Therefore, our language or expression of worship will carry a more intense response because of what God is constantly manifesting in our lives.

> The Spirit of God in me brings God an expression of worship because of my relationship and experience with Him.

We worship God in spirit and in truth, and with the experience of that truth, we bring an honest and willing worship from our inner beings. This is what I call DNA to DNA. The Spirit of God in me brings God an expression of worship because of my relationship and experience wih Him. In the impossibilities I face, and what God has brought me through, it is presented as an expression of worship I bring to Him. Every trial I am still overcoming has an expression of worship I bring to Him. It's in these trying moments I learn the names of God and the victory He brings me to.

The wonderful thing about worship is that it is universal. It is not tied to culture or status or gender; it is not tied to who we are. It's all about who God is and who He says we are. He calls us Adam. He calls us His children. He calls us redeemed. He calls us new creatures. And because of those qualities, there is an expression inside of us that only came from Him and that we can only give back to Him.

As we continue on this journey toward an appetite for worship, I want you to get prepared to enjoy the heavens as you've never enjoyed them before. Let's return to Revelation 4:8: "And the four beasts had each of them six wings about him; and they were full of eyes within: and they rest not day and night, saying, 'Holy, holy, holy, LORD God Almighty, which was, and is, and is to come.'"

When we enter into worship, it is not just about worshipping God in the here and now; worship is about worshipping God in advance. It is always about worshipping God with the future in mind, trusting Him with our future because we know His promises and His faithfulness. Knowing all He has revealed to us, we are able to worship God beyond our here and now.

"Enter into his gates with thanksgiving, and into his courts with praise: be thankful unto him, and bless his name" (Ps. 100:4). In this verse the psalmist implied that to enter through the gates to worship God, we must come with thanksgiving in our hearts. He conveyed that thanksgiving happens in two stages. First, we thank God for what He has done, and then we thank Him for what He will do, giving Him advance praise. This is modeled in the heavens through the angels surrounding the throne. As Hebrews 13:8 declares, "Jesus Christ the same yesterday, and today, and forever."

When the creatures mentioned in Revelation worshipped, they knew God is, God was, and God is to come. They don't observe time as we know it; they just know God. They know the movement of God, and there's always movement in worship, because whether we know how to say it right or do it correctly, there is a presence that captures us, a presence to which we respond. That presence draws us in to who and what God is. We see God not just in the here and now, but He enlarges our vision, our perception, of what is to come. If we only see God in the now, we may remain defeated and discouraged. But as we begin to let God enlarge our imagination, as we begin to see the God who was, is, and is to come, imagine how we will be transformed. God will do for us more than we can think or imagine.

We must become like those creatures that go around the throne. We must see God beyond our now and increase our perception of what He will do for us in the moment when we're standing before Him. We need to worship from the heavens. The Hebrew says, *Shachah Shehhah*, which means to "bow down." This denotes we have to change our posture from the sound response of worship to a posture of bowing down, which shows reverence and honor. We must change our posture and get to know God as we abandon ourselves before Him. When we give Him something to work with, when we give Him something of ourselves, we will find ourselves receiving more of Him.

SOUND DIMENSION

Consider that the original worship sound was not from instruments but was from our voices. Could it be that the sound inside of us that comes from all the pain, all the things that we've gone through, is the very sound God is looking for—that genuine expression of us? When God said, "Let us make man in our image, after our likeness" (Gen. 1:26), He breathed into man, depositing His breath inside him, giving man the ability to worship God the way God always wanted to be worshiped.

So, what is the sound dimension when it comes to worship? God moves in the sound dimension, which we see in Genesis 1:3: "And God said, 'Let there be light: and there was light.'"

We clearly see that things were created and came into existence through the voiceprint of God. God created through the sound dimension. He spoke to man through the sound dimension, and man responded and communicated back to God through his own sound dimension. Sound plays an important role in creating an atmosphere in which God moves and manifests Himself. God *shadows* Himself when the atmosphere is conducive for His glory. The very meaning of the word *image* is "shadow." Jesus gave us the beautiful picture of this when He said, "Then answered Jesus and said unto them, 'Verily, verily, I say unto you, The Son can do nothing of himself, but what he seeth the Father do: for what things soever he doeth, these also doeth the Son likewise'" (John 5:19).

I want to challenge your thinking with this statement: God moves in a sound dimension. The Bible tells us in Genesis 1:26, "And God said, 'Let us make man in our image, after our likeness: and let them have dominion over the fish of the sea, and over the fowl of the air, and over the cattle, and over all the earth, and over every creeping thing that creepeth upon the earth.'"

God spoke to Himself, and He responded in agreement to make man. It takes God to respond to God with the expression that God loves. The heavens were used to responding to the presence and movement of God. They knew God through sound.

THE CHORDS OF THE TABERNACLE

The original sound in the tabernacle was thirteen chords, not the seven we play today. The tabernacle sound was on stringed instruments, but we lost six chords when Israel was taken into Babylon and forbidden to worship.

Psalm 137:1–2 says, "By the rivers of Babylon, there we sat down, yea, we wept, when we remembered Zion. We hanged our harps upon the willows in the midst thereof." We lost the original sounds of the chords that recreated heavenly worship through the musical instruments. However, God instructed us to sing in hymns, songs, and spiritual songs (Eph. 5:19). There is always a high point in worship when the worshipper is singing in the Spirit. When we stop to listen, there is a harmony of minor chords that cannot be duplicated through instruments. God began to recreate the heavenly sound through original intent, the glory of God on our voiceprint.

Science today tells us a child recognizes his parents' voiceprint from the womb. During the later trimester of my pregnancy with Maranatha, Renny told me he loved when I fell asleep because he would speak, and Maranatha would respond to him by kicking; he would watch my stomach move in response to his voice.

Today we move to the voice of our Heavenly Father because we know the atmosphere we create for Him with our voiceprint. Once we begin a relationship with God, our Spirit-man is activated again to respond spirit to Spirit, or DNA to DNA.

BEAT, TUNE, AND RHYTHM

The sound dimension in worship is made up of beat, tune, and rhythm.

Beat. The beat sets the pace for the movement. There has to be a sensitivity to the pulse of the service or to be able to follow the instructions of the person who is leading, whether it be the worship leader, the moderator, or the preacher. The pulse of the meeting is very important.

Tune. The tune lets us know what movement we are in throughout the service. It includes the songs we are singing: praise, exaltation, worship, victory, salvation, miracles, rededication. The pulse lets us know if there is an atmosphere for miracles, deliverance, salvation, exaltation, adoration, or consecration. The preacher will know how to build from the pulse of the meeting.

Rhythm. The rhythm complements the songs we are singing. For example, we would not put a marching rhythm to an exaltation song. A marching rhythm immediately transports us into the mode of battle; an exaltation song needs strings and minor chords for us to express our hearts. The exaltation rhythm is used to create intimacy or in response to intimacy.

WHAT MUSIC SAYS ABOUT A CHURCH

We have learned to measure a church atmosphere from the worship service; we can take the spiritual temperature of a church and know the season they are in from the songs they sing in their worship experience. Charismatic churches will major in worship rather than praise songs that testify to the power of God. Pentecostal churches focus on the praise songs and have fewer worship songs. However, the larger an organization, the more they tend to major in worship songs that cater to the believers' needs rather than the songs that testify to the power and demonstration of God. The independent or nondenominational churches center on the praise songs that testify to the miraculous power of God. A combination of both worship and power-of-God songs invoke the manifestation of God's glory in our worship experience.

Congregations that like a traditional service will use hymns and spiritual songs to major in the theology of God. The emphasis is on Scripture rather than the spontaneity from the heart. How do we combine the two? The song that testifies of God and worships Him at the same time is the perfect combination—for example, "How Great Is Our God." It's both a hymn and a spiritual song, it has had different composers and song writers, and it's scriptural so it has theology. Yet it still testifies to different generations about the greatness of our God. "Amazing Grace" is another hymn that is theological, speaks of salvation, and still testifies to every generation.

You can often tell if a church majors in salvation because the songs are usually made up of "I am desperate; I need You . . . I'm running after You . . ." The emphasis is on "I" and not on "I AM." I AM is the code name for God. That was how God introduced Himself to Abraham. Genesis 15:1 says, "After these things the word of the Lord came unto Abram in a vision, saying, Fear not, Abram: I am thy shield, and thy exceeding great reward."

When a church sings a lot of breakthrough songs, their major outreach is deliverance, so their service has more praise songs than worship songs. A church that sings about the power of God often sees more miracles, because they incorporate theology and worship that set an atmosphere for God to demonstrate Himself.

6

Faith Is in the Sound Dimension of God

*So then faith cometh by hearing, and hearing
by the word of God.*
Romans 10:17

You can't define faith without mentioning the sound dimension. When we hear the Word of God, it opens up the ability to see, to believe, and to receive. God said, "Let there be light," and once it was spoken, it came into manifestation. Now we have the ability to see what He said. True faith has the ability to create because it is spoken with the authority and from God's position when He said it.

We may say, "I can see what you're saying." Our words have the ability to open up the imagination, and they synchronize our words with the spirit of the person to whom we are speaking, and there is an immediate download—the opening of the eyes to see.

Ephesians 5:19 tells us the importance of "speaking to yourselves in psalms and hymns and spiritual songs, singing and making melody in your heart to the Lord."

There is a strong emphasis on sound and the importance of the right sound and frequency in the presence of God. Our sound can do so many things in His presence. It takes faith as our foundation to discern the movement of God and faith to respond with the right sound.

Why does it take faith? Faith is the supernatural element of God that we cannot always explain with words, because it involves the unseen and can only be interpreted by the Spirit of God. The natural person will want to debate and reason us out of the moment when we are experiencing God in the now. Worship is a wonderful place to develop our faith senses and the ability to respond to the spontaneity of God.

Most people will relate to the different sounds and rhythms with their individual cultural or personal preferences. However, sound has a distinct frequency that will disarm our enemies. While the less-aware person is trying to work out what is happening, our relationship with the Lord enables us to have the right response in that now moment with God.

> The blood songs—the songs that declare the name of Jesus and the greatness of our God—affirm the dominion of territory.

We can also establish authority through the rhythm and loudness of our sound. By the loudness of sound during praise and worship, we can also identify what anointing is in the room. The dramatic or militant sound of the music should displace anything that is exalting itself or resisting the presence of God. This is most noticeable when we are doing a conference in a different city, at a new church, or at an international event. The first thing we establish is our authority in that environment. The blood songs—the songs that declare the name of Jesus and the greatness of our God—affirm the dominion of territory. There is a declaration through the songs that God is the sovereign authority in the place where we are gathering. We can't sing these songs with a gentle rhythm; it must be dramatic sound to establish the authority of God in the arena or conference.

We have used this strategy of creating a breakthrough atmosphere for years in many different worship environments. We know the importance of singing about the blood or the name of Jesus. When we sing of these two things, we remind the enemy that he is defeated, and we are reinforcing that the atmosphere and territory are in the control of our Lord and Savior. Although today we sing very few songs about the blood, this is the quickest way to set a breakthrough atmosphere for the administration of miracles.

When we first began doing crusades in London in the town hall, we would begin with songs about victory; then the blood songs for breakthrough and deliverance; then songs about God's name, or the great things about God, to build the faith of the people; and finally, the adoration or exaltation songs, which created the atmosphere of a corporate expectation for God.

We had learned this from being at the Morris Cerullo crusades in the Royal Albert Hall in London. I was a potential worship leader at that time, and God revealed to me what they were doing. This was confirmed by my husband when he gave me instructions on the flow in which he wanted the songs to go.

You can use those same principles today to establish God's authority in the meetings through the worship services.

7
Distinct Sounds

Sing aloud unto God our strength: make a joyful noise
unto the God of Jacob
Psalm 81:1

Worship involves many distinct sounds. Each has a purpose and a significance. It is important to be aware of each distinct sound so that we can recognize when each is needed.

CONFUSE OUR ENEMY

The godly sound that changes an atmosphere quickly is the use of the names of God; it always confuses the enemy. A shout of victory or praise that includes any of the names of God will confuse the enemy. Our shouts in a corporate setting show unity, faith, and power, and it will always bring about a corporate synergy and expectancy for the display of God's power. The clapping of hands in a rhythmic force will also confuse the enemy.

O clap your hands, all ye people; shout unto God with the voice of triumph. For the LORD most high is terrible; he is a great King over all the earth. He shall subdue the people under us, and the nations under our feet" (Ps. 47:1–3)

When we are worshipping together in church, we occasionally have a "praise break," which is a time of clapping of the hands. We are not clapping to call someone to us, or to get the attention of an individual; it is a clap of celebration, a clap of rejoicing. In that moment, no words have been communicated, but there is a corporate awareness of what is happening in that movement.

SOUND THE ALARM

In Scripture, the ram's horn was a curved horn used by the people and called a *shofar*. The priest used it to summon the people; the different shrill of the horn gave the people the order for that moment. The horn was used to announce the beginning and the end of the Sabbath; to gather the people if they were dispersed; to inform them of danger; to tell the soldiers to gather their arms and be ready for action; and to lead in celebration and rejoicing. And since no other nation at that time knew the shofar sound or its meaning, the sound brought terror to their enemies.

I use a shofar during our conferences to prompt the people to begin the Jericho march, which is marching in formation. I mobilize people to move in rhythm and unity with one thing in mind: we are taking this territory for the kingdom of God in our movement around the auditorium. We sing songs that make the people shout with a declaration. The shout or cheer is to let the enemy know we are coming, and we will be victorious.

I have the distinct picture of the armies coming into a territory, banging their drum in a rhythm, or the children of Israel sounding the shofar in a distinct shrill to let the army know it's time to attack. Today we no longer march into a territory; our warfare is done by planes or drones. Thus, we don't give our enemies advance warning. In our spiritual warfare, the sound still confuses the enemy. The attack is sudden and unexpected. "Blow ye the trumpet in Zion, and sound an alarm in my holy mountain: let all the inhabitants of the land tremble: for the day of the Lord cometh, for it is nigh at hand" (Joel 2:1).

DECLARE BREAKTHROUGH

When breakthrough is in the atmosphere, it comes with a sound that is loud and militant in rhythm because it acts as a hammer to break up the yokes of the people. The songs we sing establish that the administration of the presence of God is to bring about breakthrough in the lives of the audience. That militant sound also establishes authority and lets the enemy know a new kingdom has arrived. The battle and victory are easier when we establish our authority through the declaration of sound. "Is not my word like as a fire? saith the Lord; and like a hammer that breaketh the rock in pieces?" (Jer. 23:29)

When we sing songs that declare breakthrough, they are usually songs that have the Word of God or the Psalms in them. Once again, I want to reinforce that breakthrough songs are usually loud and militant to establish authority in the atmosphere.

THE SOUND OF WARFARE

I love the sound of warfare in a worship service, since I usually like a staccato sound with a militant beat mixed in. When we add songs that declare the names of God as the warrior; the power of His might; and *El Gibbor,* meaning "mighty warrior," we establish an atmosphere of expectation.

Again, let me emphasize that God moves in a sound dimension, and He uses our voices as a skillful instrument to demonstrate His power for our victory. We may choose to sing songs that call the saints into battle or about defeating the enemy, but we should always end that session with declaring the victory. We should always name the battle so we can name the victory.

"For if the trumpet giveth an uncertain sound, who shall prepare himself to the battle?" (1 Cor. 14:8).

THE SOUND OF WORSHIP

As we have already touched on, the sound of worship comes in many forms. When I think of this sound, I hear strings and wind instruments at the height of worship. The minor chords immediately establish the intimacy that testifies of our relationship with God. It also brings us back to what worship was like in the temple with the stringed instruments. The original instruments in the temple had thirteen chords, representing the original thirteen letters. Today we have seven chords, and we add to them the minor, major, diminished, augmented, and major seventh. These chords prompt us to identify with what God's presence will do. In this atmosphere, we sing about God's names: *Elohim, Elyon, El Gibbor, El-Shaddai, Jehovah-Rapha, Jehovah-Shalom, Jehovah-Tsidikenu.*

ENCOUNTERS REVEAL A NATURE OF GOD

We use the seven redemptive names of God as the foundation for our witness of God in our worship. Each of these names came about because of an encounter with God by the patriarchs in the Bible.

Jehovah-Nissi (Adonai-Nissi)—"The Lord Our Banner" (Ex. 17:8–15) Moses was given the instruction for the battle with the Amalekites, and Joshua was leading the charge in the battle. Moses held the rod as a banner for the victory that Joshua was executing. The rod symbolized the banner of the Lord in the time of battle.

Distinct Sounds

Jehovah-Rapha—"The Lord that Healeth" (Ex. 15:26) God gave a covenant to the children of Israel as a free people that would be traveling in foreign lands. If they kept the statutes and commandments of the Lord, no disease or plague would be upon them. God would be their healer.

Jehovah-Roi—"The Lord My Shepherd" (Ps. 23:1) King David understood what it was like to be a shepherd that led in dry places; there was no comfort because there was always lack. However, wherever our Good Shepherd is, there is no lack because He is the supplier of all things.

Jehovah-Shalom—"The Lord Our Peace" (Judg. 6:24) Gideon cried out to God while the nation was once again in danger of being defeated by a new nation called the Midianites. Gideon twice asked God for a sign, and when God gave him the victory he named his encounter with God, The Lord Our Peace. Today we define shalom as nothing missing, nothing lacking, and nothing broken.

Jehovah-Shammah (Adonai-Shammah)—"The Lord Is Present" (Ezek. 48:35) God spoke to Ezekiel in a vision about capturing and dividing the land for the twelve tribes of Israel. God told him specifically how to measure and divide out the land to each tribe. When Ezekiel finished dividing the territory he named the city The Lord Is Present; another translation says, The Lord Is There. God is always ahead of us in the victory!

Jehovah-Tsidkenu—"The Lord Our Righteousness" (Jer. 23:6) Israel had been a nation scattered without their own land when God told Jeremiah to declare to the people that they would again have their own land and the nation would know God as Righteousness. God has done morally right by His people again.

Jehovah-Jireh (Adonai-Jireh)—"The Lord Will Provide" (Gen. 22:13–14) Abraham took Isaac and their servants on a three-day journey to offer a sacrifice unto the Lord. While on that journey, Isaac asked of Abraham, "We have the fire and the wood. Where is the sacrifice?" Abraham declared that God would provide.

There are many other examples of encounters with God where individuals name their experience of God. My friend, that is why it is imperative that you have an intimate moment with God so that your vocabulary or expression of worship is infectious in the corporate atmosphere of His presence. "Thou art worthy, O Lord, to receive glory and honor and power: for thou hast created all things, and for thy pleasure they are and were created" (Rev. 4:11).

THE SOUND OF EXALTATION

I always imagine the sound of exaltation with strings because it denotes intimacy. We can't truly exalt God without knowing Him and being intimate with Him. To exalt God implies we are in the height of worship and everything is about His name, His character, and who He is. We must have a revelation of the Lord of hosts, the King of kings, God Almighty. Allow all the names of God to come into your vocabulary as you exalt Him.

Psalm 99:5 says, "Exalt ye the Lord our God, and worship at his footstool; for he is holy."

One illustration of exaltation I love to use is that of a nonbelievers walking into a service and getting caught up in the praise because of the rhythm, tune, or beat. They may tap their feet or clap their hands and genuinely participate in the service. However, when we begin to worship and exalt the Lord, they stand completely still and lost. Exaltation and adoration is about our personal relationship and revelation of God the Father, Jesus our Messiah, and the Holy Spirit, our helper. Exaltation is all about how we know the Lord our God, the King of kings, the Lord of lords. We are giving our witness about who He is to us.

Each of us can say we love somebody, but when the individual approaches us and asks us what we love about them, we can't give a generic answer; we must give details and examples that can only come from an intimate relationship.

Distinct Sounds

THE SOUND OF VICTORY

What does the sound of victory sound like? A jubilant people cheering, shouting, whistling, jumping, leaping, and twirling around? Victory is not just a sound; it's a posture. It's a response that is not premeditated; it's spontaneous. We have to be fully in the moment to respond. Victory songs are usually in response to knowing that the battle is won, hearing the testimony of victory, healing, deliverance, and restoration. The victory song reflects what has been defeated. This sound is usually loud and melodic. I love to use the Jewish music and rhythm to write the lyrics for our songs of victory. It brings a kingdom feel rather than a cultural feel to the worship experience.

The psalmist tells us, "O sing unto the LORD a new song; for he hath done marvelous things: his right hand, and his holy arm, hath gotten him the victory" (Ps. 98:1).

Keep in mind that we won't have all these sounds in one worship experience; however, we will begin to see the importance of being sensitive to the season and message of our church and incorporate the sounds at different times.

> The sound must correspond to the message, and the message must correspond to the revelation that is flowing from the heavens. Everyone is synchronized to the movement around the throne.

I must emphasize here that worship leaders must know the message of their leaders and write the songs that become the sound of their house. Remember, God knew when Lucifer was no longer the worship leader He created when he changed the sound that God loved to hear. All those wonderful instruments were inside of him; light exuded every time he made a sound that evoked worship in the heavens. The sound of our house should prompt the message or revelation inside the leader to come forth even more, because we have created an atmosphere that is making a demand of the revelation. The sound must correspond to the message, and the message must correspond to the revelation that is flowing from the heavens. Everyone is synchronized to the movement around the throne.

How did God know the sound in Lucifer had changed? God knew when the sound reflected the intents of Lucifer's heart and not the worship that God's presence demanded. The angels had the voiceprint of the sound. Lucifer only had the sound but not the words or voiceprint to express it. So when the emphasis became his gift and not the Giver of the gift, he could no longer keep his position as chief worship leader of the heavens.

This is a warning to worship leaders and worshippers of any congregation: when we are more caught up in our gifts and not responding to our spiritual leaders, it is time to step down. We are not leading them into God's presence to receive from Him, but we have become entertainers with wonderful gifts, instead of worshippers who are bringing the people into the corporate presence of God.

Let me touch on the Jewish sound for a moment. When we sing the psalms of David, they range from defeat, pain, abandonment, abuse, neglect, shame, rejoicing . . . You can see a wide range of emotions, and yet there is a joy in knowing the God David worships will deliver him and the nation that he is serving. The Israeli sound can take us on a rhythmic journey that will fit any culture, nationality, and tradition, because it brings a kingdom dimension to our worship experience.

8
Corporate Worship

I challenge you as you study the Word to consider how we are different from Lucifer. God doesn't want our mechanical worship; He wants the depth inside of us. Think of what He deposited when He breathed into man.

I love the visual of the number of cells inside of us—the nerves, tissues, tendons, and organs. They function inside of us, enabling us to express God beyond wood, beyond strings, beyond stones instruments.

There is a living force inside of us: God's very DNA breathed into man since Creation. That's worship. Worship is expressing every facet of ourselves in reverence to God. My friends, worship was created in the heavens, but it was perfected on the earth. He put an expression in man that is beyond the vocabulary and comprehension of the angels.

David sang in Psalm 8:2, "Out of the mouth of babes and sucklings thou hast ordained strength because of thine enemies, that thou mightest still the enemy and the avenger." Jesus later referred to this in Matthew when He says, "Yea; have ye never read, Out of the mouth of babes and sucklings thou hast perfected praise?"

Let us be a people who want praise and perfect worship to come from our mouths. Worship is in the very voiceprint that we carry when we respond to God in His presence. Even amid all our struggles—especially amid our struggles—God wants our voiceprint. He wants the sound that's inside of us to come out in worship to Him. He's not looking for how perfect it is; He's just looking for our sound, which is perfect in His ears.

The following example offers a wonderful visual of how our worship is to God. Imagine a room full of screaming, shouting children. Regardless of how crowded the room is, when they hear their parents' voices, the child doesn't turn to ask somebody, "Can you confirm that's my mom's voice? Can you confirm that's my dad's voice?" Even amid the chaos, they know their father's and mother's voices. It's typical that when a mother is in a public place and she hears "Mother," she glances around even if she knows that might not be her child; the word *mother* causes her to turn. Our heavenly Father knows our individual voices. He knows our voiceprints, and the original sound of worship is in the very sound that comes from our lips and out of our hearts. He designed us that way. I love how science confirms how unique our voiceprint and fingerprints are! The frequency of our voices cannot be matched or be identical; even twins have unique frequencies. God has put His signature inside of us to bring out the worshipper, to bring out His thoughts, to bring out His expressions.

HAVING FELLOWSHIP WITH GOD AND HEARING HIS VOICE

First Corinthians 14:10 says, "There are, it may be, so many kinds of voices in the world, and none of them is without signification." As you can tell, I am a visual person, and I realize from reading this scripture that while there are billions of people on our planet today, God knows every one of them. Science has proven that our voiceprints are unique; no two people sound the same. Every living thing that has breath is capable of praise, according to Psalms. With everything there is a

Corporate Worship

sound or distinct frequency, and our voices are significant to God. We are that important to Him; He wants to hear our expression of worship.

I challenge you to worship God with the sound that's inside you today. In Genesis we see that God made man to have fellowship with, and that relationship grew to such a point that God wanted to take that personal relationship, fellowship, and communion with Him to a more public platform. God desires corporate worship as well as personal worship. Although we don't get a description of the heavens yet, we know worship is a prominent part of the atmosphere and environment of the heavens.

In the Old Testament, we have an expression of corporate worship that God gave to Israel after they had come out of Egypt. Prior to that it was an individual expression passed down from Adam to successive generations.

> And be ready against the third day: for the third day the Lord will come down in the sight of all the people upon mount Sinai… There shall not a hand touch it, but he shall surely be stoned or shot through; whether it be beast or man, it shall not live: when the trumpet soundeth long, they shall come up to the mount… And Moses brought forth the people out of the camp to meet with God; and they stood at the nether part of the mount. And mount Sinai was altogether on a smoke, because the Lord descended upon it in fire: and the smoke thereof ascended as the smoke of a furnace, and the whole mount quaked greatly. And when the voice of the trumpet sounded long, and waxed louder and louder, Moses spake, and God answered him by a voice. (Ex. 19:11, 13, 17–19)

Don't you just love that? God responded to Moses. Moses spoke and God answered. And for the first time, a corporate body, a nation, was hearing God audibly at the same time. Incredible, right?

Imagine the amazement in a national conference if someone were to speak, whether it be a prophet, pastor, or someone in the audience, and at one time we heard God respond audibly? Now, *that* would be a worship experience—God intentionally revealing Himself, the intent of His heart, to everybody at the same time.

This encounter between God and the nation of Israel was the first time God spoke to the nation corporately; they finally had the opportunity to hear Him the same way Moses had been hearing Him since God spoke to him through the burning bush.

God began a relationship with Moses that would become the foundation of communication with the prophets and chosen leaders until Jesus was born on the earth, which changed the relationship with God and man again. I imagine God was thrilled to relate to His people in this way. God gave clear instructions how the people were to prepare themselves and approach the mountain. They heard Moses speak to God and God responding. How incredible it must have been to have a face-to-face or a voice-to-voice experience with God.

But while Moses heard God's voice, all the people heard was thunder, which was terrifying to them because they did not have a relationship with God. His voice was loud and bellowing; there was nothing inviting in His voice to them. However, Moses' relationship with God allowed him to see and hear past the lightning and thundering. A child hears his father's voice differently depending upon his relationship with his father, just as we hear God's voice differently depending upon our relationship with Him, the Creator, Master, instructor of our lives. What does God's voice sound like to you? What is your relationship with God?

CORPORATE HEARING, CORPORATE RESPONDING

God started with Adam in the garden, having fellowship with him, and it progressed until it became a nation that would hear Him and all respond at the same time. Once sin entered the human race, we could

Corporate Worship

no longer have the personal relationship with God. What was an intimate moment with Adam and Eve talking with God in the cool of the day became a corporate moment, and God spoke to a nation through a specific leader in the Old Testament. But worship is about responding to His voice, not responding to a person speaking on God's behalf.

This encounter was a national encounter and a personal one all at the same time. God went public and brought a whole nation to hear Him and respond to Him together. What a heart God had for His people! The protocol for encountering God was set in the corporate worship experience. God's intent was a nation responding to Him together, not a priest being a mediator. God's intent was a nation of worshippers.

"And ye shall be unto me a kingdom of priests, and a holy nation. These are the words which thou shalt speak unto the children of Israel" (Ex. 19:6).

Israel could not see themselves as a nation of priests and a holy nation. They still thought as slaves do, though trying to be free with a God who saw them greater than they were. Could it be that as we worship God, we often cannot break the stigma of a sin-controlled mind, which keeps us condemned in the presence of God? God called them a holy nation, He changed their identity publicly, and they could not receive it. My friend, what an injustice and a disservice we do to God when we cannot receive the identity He has declared over us. God gave a public affirmation that needed a private response from each individual. This encourages me when I am reminded that I personally must walk with God in the Spirit and not the flesh. As Paul said in Romans 8:1, "There is therefore now no condemnation to them which are in Christ Jesus, who walk not after the flesh, but after the Spirit."

At Mount Sinai, I imagine that as God spoke, or even before He spoke, the earth shook, the mountain was on fire, and smoke billowed—all because God was present. Genesis tells us that Adam and Eve heard the voice of God as He was walking in the garden (Genesis 3:8). Before they even saw Him, the earth was already responding to the sound of Him, and that's the same challenge we face today.

We want to know God in all His fullness, but some of us put restrictions on Him just like the children of Israel at Mount Sinai. When they heard His voice, fear gripped them and they argued that they preferred Moses to have the relationship with God. God could speak to Moses, and Moses could speak to them. Sadly, they were more comfortable with this distance from God. But God's sole intention is that when He speaks every person who knows Him will respond to Him. Every person who wants that relationship with Him will respect and honor Him, yielding to His will. God was present, but the Israelites weren't comfortable with that.

God is present with us as well; His voice is now. Yet people still resist His presence, declaring, "We don't want You." Can you imagine being in His presence and saying, "No, Your presence is too much for me"?

The heart of God desires to draw us in so that we can receive what He is pouring out.

The heart of God desires to draw us in so that we can receive what He is pouring out. The account in Exodus gives us that beautiful picture. The Israelites have come from being slaves, they've talked about freedom for generations and generations, and the first act of freedom is that God wants to speak to them corporately. My expression of the original intent of worship is, "I want to be with God's people, corporately in your presence, not a spectator off to one side, but corporately hearing Him at the same time, responding to Him at the same time."

Corporate Worship

In Exodus 20:1–2 God began His instruction to Moses on Sinai: "God spake all these words, saying, I am the Lord thy God, which have brought thee out of the land of Egypt, out of the house of bondage."

Notice that God introduces Himself to His people. Once He introduces Himself, and we acknowledge Him, the worship service can begin. After our acknowledgment of the Father, we are prepared to witness what He reveals. My favorite phrase is, "It takes God to introduce God." What an insult for God to introduce Himself and for us to ignore him. God introduced Himself to His people in Scripture, and they rejected Him. They preferred a man to be their mediator, when they had the distinct honor to come before Him with their petitions and be heard as a nation.

Whenever God speaks and brings us into relationship with Him, He creates a covenant with us to establish His rightful place in our lives. He always brings us a principle or a protocol of how to worship Him. Exodus 19:10–11 says, "And the Lord said unto Moses, Go unto the people, and sanctify them to day and to morrow, and let them wash their clothes, And be ready against the third day: for the third day the Lord will come down in the sight of all the people upon Mount Sinai."

God told the children of Israel that on the third day they would meet Him, and there were certain things they were and were not to do. They had two days to prepare; God called this sanctification. He told them to sanctify themselves, meaning to wash themselves and put on clean clothes, which was a representation of clean hearts. He wanted their obedience in response to Him. He wanted them to hear and respond—a corporate worship service. However, the nation did not respond the way God desired, and yet He made a covenant with them. In this covenant He established that He was their God. During worship, God establishes who we are to Him: "I am your God and you are My child." We were created in His image, after His likeness.

God then made a covenant with Israel the nation through the Ten Commandments, which He gave them through Moses. They were to have no other gods before Him. God's first act when He brought the children of Israel to Mount Sinai was to establish that He was their Source, and Provider: "I am the Lord thy God, which have brought thee out of the land of Egypt, out of the house of bondage. Thou shalt have no other gods before me" (Ex. 20:2–3).

God established His order and intent of worship so that when we come to Him, we know why we're coming and who He is. We have the revelation of who God is to us. "I am your God," He says, "and you are My people." He is our God, and we are His children. That's the New Testament; it's the old and new coming together. As His people in the twenty-first century, we know how to worship Him in the beauty of His holiness, in the counsel of His countenance. That's who He is to us: the order and intent of worship.

So now God has established how He wants us to worship Him. He teaches a nation how to draw close to Him so He can speak to them corporately, but there are different expressions of praise, which we will discuss next.

9
Acts of Praise

I want to give you a foundational truth about praise so you have something to build on and know the distinction between praise and worship. Praise and worship go together because praise affirms God's works, while worship affirms who He is. We always begin a worship service from the realm of faith. We are declaring Hebrews 11:1: "Now, faith is the substance of things hoped for, the evidence of things that are not seen."

Our worship service begins with our declaring what the evidence will be, and giving God thanks ahead of time. This is how we set an environment for miracles in our worship experience, with the declaration of faith during the praise element of our worship. Faith brings people into the power of agreement, and they begin to work that muscle of faith to see the unseen things. Yes, we describe faith as a muscle: the more you work it, the bigger and stronger it grows.

Faith works all the way through our worship service and into the ministry of the Word. Singing songs that declare the works of God in the praise element of the worship service will affirm God's power to move. The revelation and experience we have of God will allow Him to display Himself supernaturally in our service.

When we praise God, there are so many expressions that we bring. I want to share a few of them with you, their names and their meanings, so that you'll have a reference. What I really want to emphasize is our worship. It is all about bowing down and giving reverence to Him.

Alaz means "to rejoice, to exult, to jump for joy." It is most often translated "exult" or "rejoice." In Scripture, the word is found in Psalm 96:11. As referenced here, "to rejoice" is to acknowledge the Lord our God. Everything that has breath is praising Him.

Barak means "to kneel down, to bless God as an act of adoration." This word is used in Psalm 96:2 as the individual is making a public declaration of who God is to him.

Chagag means "to celebrate, to observe festival, to march in sacred procession, to be giddy, to move in a circle, to dance, to reel to and fro." This word can be found in the following scriptures: Leviticus 23:41 and Psalm 42:4. Clear instructions were given on how to worship God during the Feast of Tabernacles.

Halal means "to be clear, to shine, to boast, show, to rave, celebrate, to be clamorously foolish." The word *hallelujah* comes from this base word, which is a primary root word for "praise" in the Hebrew language. This word can be found in Psalm 150:1–3 and Psalm 149:3. The psalmist is praising God for His mighty acts, and we are to use everything around us to help make that possible—all the instruments and voices.

Halijkah means "a procession or march, a caravan; company." This word is found in Psalm 68:24, referring to the procession of the people. We love doing this as a glory march in our meetings. It's a visual way of bringing forth the breakthrough.

Karar means "to dance and whirl about." This word is found in 2 Samuel 6:14. I personally call this the priestly dance, when the leaders lead the dance of the Lord. It is also known in our ministry as the Rhema dance.

Acts of Praise

Machowl means "a round dance (chowl: whirling particles, as sand)." This word can be found in Exodus 15:20 and 1 Samuel 18:6. This dance is led by the women, singing and dancing.

Mechowlah means "a dance: company dances." Found in Exodus 15:20, these are the spontaneous songs that happen after a breakthrough or victory has occurred. I imagine this was done in Israel during the feast time. The priest would lead the dancers through the streets with the Torah in his hands.

Pazaz and *raqad* mean "to leap, to spring, as if separating the limbs." This word is found in 2 Samuel 6:16 and 1 Chronicles 15:29. It is an act of rejoicing, as when we have the victory or have overcome struggles that we've faced.

Ruwa means "to shout; to split the ears with sound; to blow an alarm (associated with trumpets)." We always recognize this sound as the shofar, or the sound that comes from our voiceprint to bring a breakthrough sound in the service.

Isaiah 54:1 gives us a visual of this: "sing O barren . . ." Make a sound that splits the ears and defy your current situation.

Shabach means "to shout, to address in a loud tone, to command, to triumph." I always see this expression as authority. We have to give volume to our voiceprint. It is an expression in the time of the high praise. This word can be found in the following scriptures: Psalm 63:1–4; Psalm 117:1; Psalm 35:27; Psalm 145:4; and Isaiah 12:6.

Shachah means "to prostate in homage or worship." I love seeing this expression and posture at the height of a worship service when there is a transition to the holiness of God's presence. This word is found in the following scriptures: Psalm 95:6; Psalm 99:5; 1 Chronicles 16:29; and Psalm 22:27.

Taqa means "to strike, to smite, or clap your hands." The clapping of the hands is associated with weapons of warfare. Depending on how we strike our hands, we can call someone, give a compliment, give honor, get someone's attention, or confuse our enemies when we're in warfare. In warfare, the striking of the hands in a rhythmic fashion lets our enemies know the strength of our weapons, causing confusion and fear among them.

Tehillah means "the singing of halals, to sing or to laud; perceived to involve music, especially singing; hymns of the Spirit." This word corresponds with Ephesians 5:19 regarding singing hymns and spiritual songs.

Towdah means "to extend the hand in adoration, avowal, or acceptance." I always call this the position or act of surrender, and shows the abandoning of oneself. The word *towdah* is derived from the word *yadah*. The usage of this word can be found in the following scriptures: 2 Chronicles 29:31; Jeremiah 33:11; Psalm 42:4; and Psalm 50:14, 23. It is used for thanking God for things not yet received, as well as things we are ready have.

These words show that worship is all about our posture when we begin to respond to His presence.

Yadah means "the extended hand, to throw out the hand, therefore to worship with hands extended." This is another posture of surrender and abandonment in the presence of the Lord. These acts always show the relationship of the worshippers and their sensitivity to the presence of God. This word can be found in the following scriptures: Genesis 49:8; 2 Chronicles 8:14; Ezra 3:10; Psalm 22:22; Psalm 69:30; 2 Chronicles 7:6; Isaiah 12:4; Jeremiah 33:11; and 2 Chronicles 20:21.

Zamar means "to pluck the strings of an instrument, to sing, to praise." It is a word largely involved with joyful expressions of music with musical instruments. Zamar often occurs at the height of worship when the strings come forth strongly over all the instruments. It is usually in the minor chords that transition us into a higher realm of worship.

All of the above are expressions of praise that begin a worship service. But when it comes to worship, there are only two meanings, which I mentioned previously. *Sagad*, "to bow down," and *proskuneo*, "to prostrate, to bend the knees." These words show that worship is all about our posture when we begin to respond in His presence. There is not only an engaging of our voiceprints, but also cooperation from our bodies.

10
Expression of Worship

It's wonderful that worship is supposed to be spontaneous. As loud and as different as all of those expressions of praise are, worship is about intimacy and spontaneity. I am very spontaneous in worship. We create an atmosphere for God's presence, and we will worship out of that presence. In a worship service, I might tell everyone to lift their hands and worship the Lord with me, singing, "Draw near with me to honor His name. I give glory to His name, the Lord Most High, the Lord my God" (spontaneous song).

I may spontaneously burst into song and put melody to the expression of my heart. It isn't rehearsed, because God loves the expression that comes out of us. *Towdah*—adoration. *Shacha*—bowing the knee. *Karar*—twirling around, dancing. That's all an expression of praise.

"I love You, Lord. You are my God. I bring my worship before You." (spontaneous song)

What about the intimacy? Again, we are putting melody to the expression inside us into the atmosphere with our voiceprint. I acknowledge that I am around the throne; I engage my heart, and everything that is within me worships Almighty God. It can be loud, it can be soft, but it's intimate because it's all about us individually responding to the very presence of God.

> **Worship began in the heavens, but it was perfected on earth through our voiceprint giving God the expressions that He loves to hear.**

I'll say it again: worship began in the heavens, but it was perfected on earth through our voiceprint giving God the expressions that He loves to hear.

THE NAMES OF GOD

As we discovered previously, wholehearted worship is what He wanted from Israel. When He showed up on Mount Sinai with that explosion of who He is, He wanted a people who would know how to respond and simply begin to praise Him, whether in dance or bowing down. Regardless of the expression, it would be exerting from their hearts. David sang in Psalm 103:1, "Bless the Lord, O my soul, and all that is within me, bless His holy name."

Isn't that a cry from the inside, aligning everything up in that spontaneous moment? No matter what my flesh feels, my spirit knows how to draw on God. Why? His DNA communicates with my DNA. The presence of God causes me to respond to the presence of God.

No matter what we're going through, worship is all about responding in the moment to acknowledge God in our presence.

Here I am, O Lord. I just want Your presence right here and now. I just want to worship You for who You are to me right now. I see Your glory

Expression of Worship

all around me. You surround me with Your love, Lord. And I worship You. (spontaneous song).

Spontaneity isn't about us presenting our needs. Spontaneity is all about us calling God by His name, saying who He is. That's why I don't just sing about needs; I sing about God the Creator, God Almighty. I love the revelation of God Almighty, the Supreme Being.

Spontaneity in worship is about knowing His name. Sometimes we may say, "Lord, You are my healer; You are my Rapha." Other times we may say, "You're Jehovah-Jireh, the God that meets my needs." But I like to call Him Elohim, Elyon. He's the Lord God, the Lord Most High, the All-Sufficient One.

Knowing God's names creates a deeper understanding of who He is. In those quiet moments when we call Him by His name, we're not calling Him for needs; we're calling Him from relationship: "I know You as my healer, but I also know You as God of the universe, my God, my Lord, my King, All-Sovereign Majesty.

What do I love about God? The answer to that question makes my worship personal. What do you love about God? What has He done for you lately for which you can sing His praises? When you answer those questions, put a melody to them, and it will become your worship song in your moment with God. The challenge is to have a new answer every day.

The book of Genesis tells us that God made man in His image, after His likeness. He made man out of the very fiber and characteristics of who He is. God is supernatural, and that's why worship was supernatural before it became natural. He wants us to understand who we are in relation to Him as He draws us into that intimate moment with Him.

Are you ready to worship and abandon yourself in Him for who He is? Do you know the characteristics that God possesses that enable you to give Him worship from the realm of heaven rather than your natural feelings based on the circumstances in your life? Those may be difficult questions to answer.

We need to examine how we can relate with God, what can initiate the high praise or worship from the depths of our spirit. We can only worship God when we know He is above our circumstances, and our present trials are not a reflection of who He is. Worship must always acknowledge God as our source in our lives.

Faith is a crucial part of expressing worship. I am reminded of my children when they were younger and were learning to make decisions and requests for things, especially when we went shopping. They couldn't read the price tags or discern the amount of change I had in my purse. Notice I said change. Yet their eyes had no price tag awareness! All they knew was that Mom or Dad supplied for their needs. They only had to ask, and it could happen right there. My children did not have to understand faith; because of relationship they knew it was our duty or responsibility to supply. We were the only source they knew, so they asked for things out of innocence.

When we have a relationship with God, we will discover that it is His good pleasure to supply all our needs. Faith is a given if you are in good standing with Him; relationship will always include faith: "In whom we have boldness and access with confidence by the faith of him" (Eph. 3:12).

As my children grew, their needs and the price tags became greater as they began to discover purpose. Now they must learn responsibility and accountability to receive from their higher Source, God. As we mature, our purpose requires faith; our purpose is based on the seeds God has sown inside of us, and by His plan and purpose it will come to pass. God meets our needs, but we have to work and sow toward purpose. Greatness is inherent in us because of the DNA of God inside of us. However, through faith we work, and God enables purpose to become evident in our lives.

As a child grows and his needs become more than what can be met by his parents, he begins to take on responsibility. With responsibility comes the working of his faith to be able to see more than having his

Expression of Worship

needs met. Purpose will always drive us to work out our faith and believe for the unseen things God has put into our spirits.

Hebrews 11:6 says, "But without faith it is impossible to please him: for he that cometh to God must believe that he is, and that he is a rewarder of them that diligently seek him." As we mature in our Christian walk, we get to the stage in our lives when we walk to please God, rather than seeking His good pleasure to please us. Maturity uses our faith to please God, providing evidence of His good works. This is proof of growth. We begin to move from a supply-all-my-needs-without-me-doing-anything relationship to one in which our responsibility is the growing of our faith. Maturity is evidence of an active faith walk.

I cannot imagine my grown children only wanting their needs met by my husband and me and not having the maturity to boast of their faith at work in their lives. Scripture tells us that faith without works is dead (see James 2:17). Maturity wants works to show off their God. What do you desire? Your needs being met and no more? Or the demonstration of faith in God in any circumstance? Faith for a breakthrough that will enlarge me further in my spiritual growth.

Worship will always bring us into a greater awareness of who God is and our relationship with Him. Our worship will transform us in the presence of God. Not until we abandon ourselves do we find ourselves in God. We must be more God-conscious in those spontaneous moments with God to capture the fullness of Him with us.

Immaturity will keep us living from one moment to the next, always in a need-driven state. Worship will break the boundaries of limitation and bring us boldly to God's throne to be enlarged and renewed in our thoughts and hearts. Lack of faith will keep us living from paycheck to paycheck, continually in a cycle of need. Faith will make us sow seeds and believe in God for the future. Worship will fortify our minds to receive the evidence of things for which we are hoping.

11
Personal Revelation

Have you received clues about who Jesus is but have not voiced your understanding yet? Let's look at Simon Peter and see how he related to Jesus differently than the other disciples. He saw clues the others overlooked.

It became very apparent that Peter saw Jesus in a different way than the others did when Jesus gave them instructions to meet Him on the other side of the sea. They took a leisurely cruise at night to give them plenty of time to relax before Jesus arrived.

> And in the fourth watch of the night Jesus went unto them, walking on the sea. And when the disciples saw him walking on the sea, they were troubled, saying, It is a spirit; and they cried out for fear. But straightway Jesus spake unto them, saying, Be of good cheer; it is I; be not afraid. And Peter answered him and said, Lord, if it be thou, bid me come unto thee on the water. And he said, Come. And when Peter was come down out of the ship, he walked on the water, to go to Jesus. (Matt. 14:25–29)

It excites me to read and visualize this scripture in a different way. My questions to provoke you to think are, who is Jesus to you? What do you know and love about Him?

If we asked that question to the disciples in the boat, we would still have the same outcome: only Peter would answer, "Bid me come." He was having an inner experience that kept being confirmed by the supernatural things he witnessed.

In the midst of all his fellow disciples' fears and questions, Peter had an inner witness for which he did not yet have a vocabulary. He was willing to be a participant in the supernatural. He was willing to step out of his comfort zone and being one of the majority. They saw but they didn't see; they were reactionary, not responding to the moment. They saw caution, while Peter needed confirmation.

Let me give you another example of Peter discovering who Jesus was to him personally. In Matthew 16:13 we read, "When Jesus came into the coasts of Caesarea Philippi, he asked his disciples, saying, Whom do men say that I the Son of man am?"

When reading this account of Jesus with the disciples in Caesarea Philippi, it helps to know the history of the place in order to understand why Jesus was asking that question. There are so many interesting facts about this city. This was the location of the Cave of Pan, the place of the pagan Gate of Hades (gate of hell). It was the area where King Jeroboam led the Northern Kingdom of Israel into idolatry. This was also the place where the Greeks and Romans received revelations from the god Pan, who was considered a seer, or fortune teller.

When Jesus asked the disciples this question, I can imagine the debate that took place among them before they answered. In their debate, they repeated what they had heard the crowd or multitudes that followed Him say. "And they said, some say that thou art John the Baptist: some, Elias; and others, Jeremias, or one of the prophets" (Matt. 16:14).

Personal Revelation

They had been with Jesus and seen some phenomenal miracles and heard great teaching with such authority; and yet, when He asked them a question, they gave Him the people's answer. They were so caught up in the moments of miracles and the daily schedule, they did not take the time to discover for themselves who Jesus was. You will see later in the discussion that Simon had a different mindset about how he saw Jesus.

If we don't know who Jesus is, how can we worship Him?

If we don't know who Jesus is, how can we worship Him?

Notice that what they repeated from the people was a reference point from history; the disciples had nothing current with which to compare Jesus. He was a complete mystery to them.

Surely they remembered the previous miracles of the five loaves and two fish, as well as the demon-possessed child being delivered. They could recall the prophets they had heard the people compare Jesus to, but none of those prophets had done miracles for the ordinary people as Jesus did. The blind saw; the deaf heard; the lame walked; lepers were healed—these were just a few of the evidences they could recall.

However, at the height of the discussion Simon answered, "'Thou art the Christ, the Son of the living God.' And Jesus answered and said unto him, 'Blessed art thou, Simon Barjona: for flesh and blood hath not revealed it unto thee, but my Father which is in heaven'" (Matt. 16:16–17)

What does it take to have a revelation of Jesus? It takes an encounter with the Father, but we have to be willing participants. While the other disciples were involved in the discussion, Simon Peter had a willing spirit; he did not get caught up in their arguments.

Once Simon Peter made that declaration, Jesus gave him his new name, purpose, and mandate. "And I say also unto thee, That thou art Peter, and upon this rock I will build my church; and the gates of hell shall not prevail against it" (Matt. 16:18).

We must have our own encounters with God, Jesus, and the Holy Spirit to express ourselves in His presence.

I have preached from this chapter as have so many before, but I suddenly noticed something about the revelation Peter received from the Father. Peter is in the same environment, in the same city with all the distractions as the other disciples; he could repeat the same answers the people gave in their discussions about Jesus. But Peter chose to hear God privately in a public setting. His revelation of Jesus was never voiced by the other disciples. There is no written evidence that they repeated Peter's answer or that they acknowledged it. It is not recorded that the disciples had the same revelation or experience as Peter did. In other words, Peter's revelation did not persuade them to know Jesus in that way.

Peter's witness of Jesus was that he now knew how to express who Jesus was to Jesus, but that did not make the disciples have the same testimony. We must have our own encounters with God, Jesus, and the Holy Spirit to express ourselves in His presence.

"Wherefore I give you to understand, that no man speaking by the Spirit of God calleth Jesus accursed: and that no man can say that Jesus is the Lord, but by the Holy Ghost." (1 Cor. 12:3).

Personal Revelation

Father, I lift up the readers of this chapter to You
in the name of Jesus.
Father, You know that they have been struggling
to express who You are to them.
They can quote what other people say of You,
but right now give them an encounter with You
that allows them to express who You are to them.
Let them know the healing truth that is in Your Word,
Your Name, and the Spirit of the living God.
We declare an encounter with You today
that will touch every area of their lives, in Jesus' name.
Remove all fear, all doubt, all false imagination
and wrong confessions, in Jesus' name.
Let them have victory today and
begin to see the evidence of it.
Thank You, Father.

12
Supernatural Worship

What is the evidence of supernatural worship? Pause and think about that for a moment.

Every aspect of worship contains prayer, worship, and the Word. There is always a marrying of the three; they are mixed differently in different formats, yet they produce worship. So, what is the evidence of supernatural worship?

When we worship, we know that we're calling on God's name; it is coming out of a place of intimacy and our relationship with Him. The evidence of supernatural worship always releases miracles, always releases the glory of God, always establishes an atmosphere where God is free to display Himself.

In worship, we discover the three realms of the supernatural: faith, the anointing, and the glory of God.

FAITH

We always start a service in faith, with an unknown song written on the spot. My inspiration always comes from the intercessor prayer led by Mama Billie and Papa Al Deck, our spiritual parents. I will sing out of the presence that's being built from the prayer service at the beginning of our meetings. In our worship service, some of the songs are spontaneous, and while some of them are prewritten, there's always that element of faith that causes us to step out into the unknown.

We start in the faith realm declaring what we are expecting and anticipating to receive from the service. We also sing those songs that will set the atmosphere for expectancy. The songs will mention the power of God, victory, the blood, as well as the names of God. We will not be singing about our needs, or our circumstances. Those types of songs keep the focus on us and the immediate relief we need from God. To build an atmosphere of faith, however, we must sing about the attributes of God and not focus on our lives.

Singing faith-building songs informs the audience that they are not in their regular church service: they have already come into a miracle preparation environment. The atmosphere is set through the songs, the response of the people, and being in one accord through the declaration of the songs.

Colossians 3:16 tells us, "Let the word of Christ dwell in you richly in all wisdom; teaching and admonishing one another in psalms and hymns and spiritual songs, singing with grace in your hearts to the Lord."

This type of service is the example of not singing hymns, but spiritual songs that quote the Word of God. We start off spontaneously so that we can build to the anointing. To explain it another way: I like to start where we will end up; we start in the unknown to end up in the unknown display of God.

THE ANOINTING

The anointing breaks the yoke, so we sing particular songs about God's power, His blood, and His greatness, because that sets the atmosphere for the anointing to work. There's still the element of faith working. These songs establish the spiritual authority in the environment and an atmosphere for God to demonstrate Himself. The anointing breaks the "I's" that we have brought into the service: I'm sick, I'm depressed, I'm in debt, I'm hungry.

This is the part of the service where we identify what heaviness or burden the people have carried in that must be broken off in order to see the glory of God. This is when we sing the breakthrough songs, songs about victory and overcoming, declaring our increase and overtaking blessings. We begin to sing about the acts of God and His promises concerning us. The songs of the anointing usually carry a militant sound to establish the authority of God in the service.

"And it shall come to pass in that day, that his burden shall be taken away from off thy shoulder, and his yoke from off thy neck, and the yoke shall be destroyed because of the anointing" (Isa. 10:27).

When people have carried yokes or burdens for a long time, they carry a weight in the atmosphere, that, when they walk into a room, a sensitive person can feel. Can you imagine a room filled with believers who each come in carrying a heavy yoke? We cannot sing a song about bringing awareness to that burden. We have to sing a song about the power of God, the victory of God in their lives to overcome and break off the weight of that burden. That's why breakthrough songs are usually joyful, full of drums, with a militant beat or warfare sound. I usually see this as mobilizing an army for victory! Again you are bringing everyone in one accord, those with burdens and those who can rejoice because they have had their burdens removed; everyone sings one song of victory together.

THE GLORY

This is the point in the service when there's a whole different level because of the glory—it is all about His name and His presence; it's about God displaying Himself.

Glory means the self-evident presence of God in the now. The songs that we sing about the glory always testify to who God is, what

God has done, and what He will do. We always sing about His name, and the revelation of His name to each of us. In the height of glory in our services, I love singing, "I know You. . . ." I add to that how I know Him; what is my witness of Him in my life? That's the height of intimacy.

The glory has a different atmosphere than that of faith and the anointing in worship. The glory of God really manifests when everything is in place in a service. You can't choreograph the glory of God, or have a method, such as three praise songs, two worship songs, and then the glory. The glory is all about creating the atmosphere for the presence of God.

Preachers have their own particular songs they love to hear before they minister. The service is geared for their style of ministry and administration. However, when it comes to setting the atmosphere for the glory of God, I love the expression "I have no control," because suddenly the order of songs has changed, there is a height that demands either a response or a song that is not on the list. Spontaneity takes place, and because of relationship with the Lord, we have to respond out of the atmosphere that has been created.

A worship leader who will sing spontaneously is an asset to a preacher. The preachers can administrate by what they have discerned is in the atmosphere, or they are given the word of knowledge to minister what they did not preprogram. This is an amazing moment, because it requires us to be sensitive to the presence of God, rather than depending on our gifts or callings.

When we worship, we have those sweet elements: faith, the anointing, and the glory of God. We always start our meetings in faith, declaring what we are expecting to see; the anointing establishes the kingdom of God for His display of breakthroughs; and the glory is the demonstration of God doing whatever we have created the atmosphere for Him to do. We promote audience participation through declaration moments, declaring, "You are going to receive your miracle tonight!" Faith always declares the end from the beginning. We declare at the beginning what we expect to see God do at the end of the service.

MISSISSIPPI AND COLORADO

I will never forget doing a meeting in Mississippi years ago. I was ministering in song and kept singing, "Release me," over and over again. As I was singing that, I felt a myriad of angels in the room, and they were using my song to encourage the people to come into agreement to release the angels to work on their behalf. That night when we took testimonies, people received healing in their bodies, miracles in their stomachs, and answered prayers for job positions.

I realized by being open to God in the administration of what He is saying in the moment, or the movement of His presence, He can do multiple things beyond the spiritual gift that I operate in. The key is being open to God's administration of His presence. When I can be focused on only one need, God is able to do multiple things out of the same atmosphere.

The anointing is all about breaking the yoke.

We are declaring the evidence before we have it in our hands. The anointing is all about breaking the yoke. It's important to use the sound dimension strategy in our services to get the full impact of the glory for the demonstration of our God.

I remember doing the worship in a meeting in Colorado. The pastor told us a couple who needed a miracle was coming to the meeting. Dr. Renny and I were not told of their condition until afterward. While I was leading worship, I began to sing, "Step, step into the glory . . ."

The husband told us afterward that because they had traveled a long way, he had left his wife in the room sleeping in her wheelchair while he had come down to the service. While I was singing that spontaneous song, I had people doing the glory march around the ballroom. In the line that passed me was this man's wife. She got out of her wheelchair, took off her oxygen, and ended up singing with me at the front.

Glory to God! For the husband, the first time he realized that his wife was not in the hotel room, and she was healed was when he heard and saw her singing with me at the front of the ballroom.

In worship we create an atmosphere where a person can witness the blind see, the deaf hear, and the lame walk, because usually that's the anointing on the man or the woman of God, so they know they're anointed in a specific burden for a specific need. But when it comes to the glory, that is all about God. We don't know what to expect. In one moment, we may have people being healed, people being delivered, people seeing into the heavens because God is on display. We have no control over what God is getting ready to do, but will we have faith to trust Him?

13
Prophetic Worship

Then sang Deborah and Barak the son of Abinoam on that day, saying, Praise ye the LORD for the avenging of Israel, when the people willingly offered themselves. Hear, O ye kings; give ear, O ye princes; I, even I, will sing unto the LORD; I will sing praise to the LORD God of Israel. (Judg. 5:1–3)

It amazes me that Old Testament prophets didn't have a script; they didn't have written lyrics to start singing about what God had done. Their worship had to be supernatural; it had to be spontaneous.

In Judges we have a prophet who happens to be a woman, and neither prophets nor women were sent to battle. Here we have a general who—because of the Word of the Lord—is willing to take the risk to go to battle with a prophet who happens to be a woman.

In her song, Deborah declares her authority: "Hear, O kings and princes." She established the right to face principalities and powers.

Did you notice they started singing before they had the victory? That is supernatural worship! Or consider the account we looked at earlier, when the Israelites crossed over the Red Sea and Moses began to sing. "Then Moses and the Israelites sang this song to the LORD:

"I will sing to the Lord, (the same line) for he is highly exalted. Both horse and driver he has hurled into the sea" (Ex. 15:1 NIV).

Once again, there was no script, no prerecorded song for this moment of victory. The prophets had no frame of reference, so they had to respond to God with their vocabulary in this wonderful moment of victory.

I can just see Miriam excited as she sang her heart out with the people and her brother, unable to keep her body from dancing. "Then Miriam the prophet, Aaron's sister, took a timbrel in her hand, and all the women followed her, with timbrels and dancing. Miriam sang to them: 'Sing to the Lord, for he is highly exalted. Both horse and driver he has hurled into the sea'" (Ex. 15:20–21 NIV)

Again, these songs weren't prerecorded or premeditated, and the dance wasn't choreographed. These elements of worship were spontaneous. Today we call it the Rhema dance, the dance of the spirit. It comes immediately by responding to a "God moment." It gives God an expression that is not our usual form of worship.

Every generation will have a different testimony about how great our God is.

In worship there is always a progression from faith to anointing to the glory of God. Though we may fail to recognize the progression or to name it, there's always a progression. We might start off singing one of my favorite praise songs, "How great is our God. Sing with me, how great is our God." It's a wonderful praise song, because as David said, every generation will have a different testimony about how great God is. "Now also when I am old and greyheaded, O God, forsake me not; until I have shewed thy strength unto this generation, and thy power to every one that is to come" (Ps. 71:18). Every song we sing should be a song that testifies about who God is in our now.

Every generation will have a different testimony about how great our God is. For those of us old enough to remember, one version went, "Then sings my soul, my Savior God to Thee. How great Thou art!"

As we're moving in the presence of God and believing God for miracles in an atmosphere where He is present, we can see God doing things beyond our imagination. However, the song has to reflect the movement of God's presence.

Ephesians 5:19 commends us, saying, "Speaking to yourselves in psalms and hymns and spiritual songs, singing and making melody in your heart to the Lord."

Many think that hymns are old school. Some of us will say, "I don't even know any hymns." That's fine. Years ago, many people could not read, and they didn't have their own personal copy of the Bible, so the priest or spiritual leaders had to devise a way for the congregation to know theology (the Word of God). Songwriters wrote the Scriptures and put melody to them, creating hymns.

Spiritual songs were written in every culture to express their vocabulary and rhythm. The songs became traditional to every nation, culture, and people. Some of the spiritual songs transcended different cultures and became popular, but many songs remain within the culture and became traditional. African Americans have their spirituals; people of the Caribbean have their spiritual songs; the denominational churches have their liturgical songs; and the Israelites wonderful psalms.

But then there are the songs of the Spirit, songs that are written in the moment. This is the spontaneous worship in response to God. We've seen in our own meetings times when we are singing, and as we're singing people are being healed. That's not a hymn, and that's not from our cultural spiritual song; that's from the song of the moment.

I remember the first time we did a worship service in London, and Dr. Renny told the worship team and me that miracles were going to break out that night. We said that was wonderful; we were used to seeing that. But he continued, "No, it is going to break out before I even speak." We prepared the audience, telling them to turn and tell their neighbor, "My miracle is going to be greater than yours."

We started singing the known songs, and while in the middle of singing, a lady got up out of her wheelchair. The place erupted; the people were so excited. My heart was pounding because I thought it was too early in the service. I began to think, *What songs are we going to sing now?*

And so we did what every worship leader does when they don't know what to do; we told people, "Lift your hands in His presence and just begin to praise Him right where you are."

There's a spontaneity when the order of service has changed. Think about that. The order of service has changed, so now we can't go with what's written; we have to go with what the Spirit is saying and doing. I couldn't tell you the song I wrote in that moment. All I know is out of that presence we began singing a new song, and to this day I'm still singing new songs because worship has the evidence of the supernatural in it.

I tell worship leaders all the time, sing what's in your spirit.

God makes us respond to Him with a rhythm, in the moment, in the movement that His spirit is moving.

YOUR SONG OF VICTORY

My friends, the evidence of supernatural worship is you don't go by what's written on the screen or by another songwriter. Instead, you go by what is written in your spirit. You don't go by what's spoken audibly by everyone around you; you go by what is spoken to your spiritual ears that are hearing the Spirit of God.

Let me explain that. I tell worship leaders all the time, to sing what's in their spirits. When you get into that height where you've sung all the "hallelujahs" you know to sing, you have sung all the "We exalt Thee, O Lord," then sing what's in your spirit.

And as we sing what's in our spirits, we are writing the song of the Spirit that becomes the song of our house. You might say to me, "I'm not a worship leader, Dr. Marina; why would I want to sing a new song?"

As you lie on your bed, become like David: "I speak of the things which I have made touching the king: my tongue is the pen of a ready writer" (Ps. 45:1).

Start to tell the Lord, as David did, all the things God has done for you, the situations He has brought you through, the unmerited favor you have gained. Your response will keep getting longer because of the power of recall going on within. Start with how you feel. *Oh, Lord, today was just a horrible day.* Then put a melody to it. *Lord, help me today. You know how defeated I feel.*

Tell Him how you feel; He can handle it. But once you tell Him how you feel, you've got to grab hold of His name and declare, "You are a great God. You can deliver me because You've done it before, O mighty God, You can bring me out. You can bring me out."

Then use His name: *You are El Gibbor, Almighty Warrior. You can fight on my behalf. If I'm in dire straits, You are my shalom, my peace. You rest over me right now; You create my environment for peace.*

Yes, sing your song of victory!

What did you just do? You broke out of how weak and fragile you are in the comfort of your home and in the comfort of your place. You just changed your mind and your imagination. You just renewed your spirit by changing your focus from your bad day to focusing on your God, the God who overcomes.

I ask you, what is the evidence of supernatural worship? It is you moving your mind-set from what your circumstance says and moving your whole being, calling your whole being into alignment to what God is saying and what God is doing.

Perhaps you are wondering how you write songs for your church that will reflect the supernatural.

Listen to what your man or woman of God is speaking on. If they're speaking about miracles, write the supernatural songs about miracles on which your man or woman of God is speaking. Use their vocabulary to write the songs. Whatever season they are teaching, write the songs of that season.

You will create the atmosphere in your church, and that song will become the song and sound of the house.

I've learned to write the songs of my apostle because I know that when people have heard his word and his teaching, it has left an impression on them. And as they start to sing those songs, it solidifies the Word and the teaching in their hearts.

Psalm 100:4 declares, "Enter into his gates with thanksgiving, and into his courts with praise: be thankful unto him, and bless his name." But the verse preceding it, verse 3, says, "Know ye that the Lord he is God: It is he that hath made us, and not we ourselves; we are his people, and the sheep of his pasture."

You've come with me, but just before we enter into His gates, what is your relationship with the Lord? Do you know Him as the Lord your God? I want to challenge you that when you enter His gates, you know that He is the Lord your God, and you already know what He is able to do for you. The psalmist tells us, or gives the impression, that when we worship God, when we enter into His gates, we are worshipping Him in advance, with foreknowledge, in expectancy. There are songs that we sing that take us from the outer court to the inner court and then into the Holy of Holies. Three different kinds of songs are needed because there are three different mind-sets as we enter His gates. Worship involves the posture of how we enter in and the different movements of God.

Prophetic Worship

When we are just entering His gates, there are songs we sing that tell us that we are just beginning that entrance, we are just beginning to get our mind-set going. We are in the outer courts.

When we enter His gates, we are coming into His presence, singing, "Come, now is the time to worship," and similar songs. They let us know we are entering into the inner court. Our songs are all about preparing our flesh for Him, declaring our hunger and thirst for His presence. We are preparing our bodies as living sacrifices.

As we enter the Holy of Holies, the songs are not about our flesh. Our songs are all about our revelation of the God we serve. How do we know God? King David knew Him as God Almighty, the God of the universe, the God of his salvation. He wrote about these revelations in his psalms, or songs, unto the Lord. They were his personal testimony of God that the nation of Israel sang too. It was rehearsed through the generations, and we sing those songs today. David's "Holy of Holies" experience of worship inspires us to write our songs of how we know God and express it in our worship time to him.

14
Living Sacrifice

I beseech you therefore, brethren, by the mercies of God, that ye present your bodies a living sacrifice, holy, acceptable unto God, which is your reasonable service.
Rom. 12:1

Becoming a living sacrifice is about our dying to self, putting to death all that glorifies the flesh, and gaining a hunger for things of the Spirit. We're no longer focused on the songs where the emphasis is all about us. We know when we're in the inner courts because all our songs are typically about our needs, and they satisfy our emotions. The inner court is about the preparation of our flesh.

In a sense we become the Old Testament priest that inspected the sacrifice to make sure there was no blemish or disease on the animal that would be sacrificed. The priest checked the animal's organs for purity. When the organs were put on the altar with the fat, there was a fragrance and intensity of heat that promoted a good sacrificial fire from earth to heaven. God wants us to use the Holy Spirit to fillet the dead things from our lives, so that we can be purified by the fire of God in worship. We become the sacrifice that is made perfect in

His presence. The Holy Spirit performs surgery that cuts away the impurities that we have held onto that are baggage in our lives. But they are only highlighted as baggage when we lay ourselves willingly on the altar to be a living sacrifice.

My husband describes *holy* as "cut apart and separated." The challenge God is calling the worshipper to today, is being holy, cut and separated for God's use.

Leviticus 1:9 tells us, "But his inwards and his legs shall he wash in water: and the priest shall burn all on the altar, to be a burnt sacrifice, an offering made by fire, of a sweet savor unto the Lord."

I sometimes imagine in the height of worship dead flesh being presented to God corporately to bring about a sweet-smelling savor of worship unto the Lord. We associate washing with water in the tabernacle as being washed in the Word of God. Therefore, I always emphasize that we cannot be true worshippers without knowing the Word of God. That is what keeps us pure, in your daily walks of prayer, the Word, and worship.

Romans 12:1 tells us, "Present your bodies as a living sacrifice." All of the attention is on our flesh, so we sing songs about being desperate and hungry for the Lord. Those are the inner court songs, but they don't exactly bring the fullness of the presence of God. They are just preparing us for the Holy of Holies.

But once we enter the Holy of Holies, the songs change. They are not about coming to worship or hungering for Him. They are all about the presence. One of my favorite old songs says, "All heaven declares the glory of the risen Lord." When we start to sing about the heavens, we have moved past "Come, let us enter." We have moved past "I am hungry for You, Lord." We have moved into the beauty and the sovereignty, the majesty and the kingship of the Creator and Master of our lives. We're moving into His name, and in His name is His power.

As I mentioned earlier, praise affirms God's works, but worship affirms God's name. We cannot sing about His name without expecting the supernatural to show up, especially when we've created an environment that is all about the declaration of who He is. When we enter into His gates, we come in with an expectancy if we know who He is to us. We have prepared our bodies and minds and have laid all the foundation. Worship is now about Him and the Holy of Holies experience of God making Himself public, that Sinai experience.

We've come, we've all prepared ourselves, but we're coming to hear Him audibly, see Him move publicly together, and that's the acceleration that happens in a service when everybody is on the same page, when we're all pouring our hearts out unto Him. The living sacrifice is in unity before the throne of the Lord in worship. When the heavens declare, the earth responds. I love that the heavens begin to speak, and the earth responds to Him. We are the earth; we are the flesh that He blew His breath into and commanded us to worship. Corporately we enter into His gates, enter into God's moment together. That's what this is about.

The evidence of worship, the evidence of supernatural worship, the evidence of our pouring ourselves out is manifested through praise affirming God in this atmosphere of electrifying worship. There is a height with all of these corporate voices. We give God worship, and He gives us His glory. We've prepared our flesh; it is now dead. We've prepared our thoughts; they are centered on our revelation of who He is. Our hearts are responding to everything He is doing in that moment.

We are the earth; we are the flesh that He blew His breath into and commanded us to worship.

This supernatural worship brings forth the display of miracles. The sickness in my body is healed. The new organs that I need—creative miracles take place in the atmosphere of glory. Eyes that are dim begin to see. Deaf ears hear; lame legs walk. Why? Because of the presence of God that is flowing as we worship.

Lift your hands right now and enter into that realm. Oh, hallelujah, hallelujah, hallelujah! We have drawn God's ear, and He listens to our hearts, not laying out the need, but saying His name. Oh, just say it with me, whatever name of God you know, say that right now. To me right here in this moment He is El Shaddai, more than enough; I am in expectancy of an acceleration of God's provision in my life. For you where you are, the revelation that He is your healer, Jehovah-Rapha, may be what you need in this moment of your worship experience. If you are in torment in your worshipping now, He is Jehovah-Shalom, your peace. If you are worn out, He's Jehovah-Tsidikenu, your righteousness.

O, hallelujah! Some of you who need life, He's Jehovah-Rohi, breathing life into you. And for some of you, He's Jehovah-Shammah, the God that sees, the God that's there; God got there ahead of you, and He's been waiting for you to get into His time frame. Perhaps He's Jehovah-Yada, the God that knows. Whatever it is you hear in your spirit-man, say it out loud. Create a melody about it right now. O, hallelujah, hallelujah. Worship Him right where you are. Sing your song. Mine is, *"El Shaddai. You are my El Shaddai. You're more than enough for me, O God. You are the many-breasted one, everything I need You can supply. You are more than I can think or imagine or believe, and that is why I worship You, I worship You, O God."*

God is the Author of the law of exchange. He gave us the rhythm of breathing in and exhaling from the first breath He breathed into man. He also taught us that worship is like a vapor or sweet-smelling aroma that He loves. In the book of Leviticus God told the priests the various sacrifices that He would accept on the altar:

> And if his offering be of the flocks, namely, of the sheep, or of the goats, for a burnt sacrifice; he shall bring it a male without

Living Sacrifice

blemish. And he shall kill it on the side of the altar northward before the Lord: and the priests, Aaron's sons, shall sprinkle his blood around about upon the altar. And he shall cut it into his pieces, with his head and his fat: and the priest shall lay them in order on the wood that is on the fire which is upon the altar: But he shall wash the inwards and the legs with water: and the priest shall bring it all, and burn it upon the altar: it is a burnt sacrifice, an offering made by fire, of a sweet savor unto the Lord. (Lev. 1:10–13)

God set out the protocol of how to present a living sacrifice to Him and how the priest should receive it and prepare before it went on the altar. This was the Old Testament principle; in the New Testament God gave us a different instruction. He requires a living sacrifice that is no longer an animal, but humankind in a constant process of being made holy.

Again, as Romans 12:1 tells us: "I beseech you therefore, brethren, by the mercies of God, that ye present your bodies a living sacrifice, holy, acceptable unto God, which is your reasonable service."

As living sacrifices, our worship is an aroma God cannot resist; it gets His attention every time. God gives us His attention; and because of the law of exchange, we give Him worship, and His response is to exhale His glory.

God will always manifest Himself when He sees that we obey His commands with the right form of sacrifice. God wants us. And right where we are we can let God manifest His presence. Let Him know that He is received right here and right now. You are in a face-to-face moment with God. Release your worship; release your sound.

Move now from your outer court into the Holy of Holies with your God, and that is the evidence of supernatural worship. My heart is that your worship experience will change, and you will know all of the different facets that make up the worshipper. You will know how to create an atmosphere, and how to respond to God from your heart. Whatever posture you give Him, you know that He will respond to you.

Keep in mind the three kinds of songs:

- The outer court songs are the preparation to thanksgiving unto the Lord. They are acknowledging who God is. Examples are songs that welcome the Holy Spirit; prepare this place for worship; and declare that this is holy ground.

- Next, we move to the inner court songs, which speak about salvation, healing, the condition of our lives, trusting God, the greatness of God, the power of God. These are faith-building songs, songs about what we are expecting God to do in the service.

- And finally, we sing the songs for the Holy of Holies. These are the songs about the names of God, God's attributes and character, and our relationship and revelation of Him. God displays Himself strongly in our Holy of Holies–style worship. The only agenda on our hearts and in the atmosphere is God, not fleshly motives.

It's been a treat taking you into my heart for worship, my experience with worship. I've been a worshipper for over thirty-five years, working with Dr. Renny, so I know the mistakes, but I also know the joy of pouring myself out unto the Lord and watching you, the audience, respond on that journey with me as the heavens open.

So my prayer is that as you've been reading, the heavens have opened up for you, and you realize the atmosphere of heaven right there in your room or wherever you are sitting, you recognize there is now a new presence of God that you identify because your heart has been changed into a worshipper. Pray with me,

Father, I thank You for teaching my heart,
my voice, my imagination, my whole being
to respond to You in Your realm.
Thank You for letting me experience the heavens
right here in the atmosphere of where I am.
Thank You for letting me share my voiceprint
and receiving me in the heavenly realm.
I know that I'm responding to heaven and
heaven is responding to me as
I have become and am becoming a worshipper.

15
My Testimony

If you could have had a conversation with my mom, she would have told you I started singing from a young age with the songs on the radio. However, as I got older, I sang in the youth choir, the adult church choir, the school choir, and Morris Cerullo crusade choir.

I've sung at the prestigious Southwark Cathedral, Royal Albert Hall, and various town halls, singing solo and with conference choirs in the United Kingdom.

The late Charles Headlam, my dad and pastor, would use me as his back-up worship leader when the designated person was late. I later saw this as training to work with my husband, who loves giving me the challenge of being ready to take over a song he has spontaneously started.

My training as a worship leader began at eighteen, working with my husband as his main worship leader. Though he was tough, he knew we had to create an environment that was not traditional in order to lead people into the presence of God for the meetings we began to do outside our church walls.

I grew up singing hymns from the *Redemption Hymnal,* choruses from song sheets, consecration songs from the sacred song booklet that would set the tone of the service. But because of the types of meetings we were doing, my husband wanted choruses that had the names of God, or blood songs that would create a power atmosphere and not a traditional church service atmosphere, or songs that would testify to the power of God. You might call it a camp-style service rather than a traditional church worship experience. He wanted songs that would build the believers' expectancy for miracles, rather than songs that would minister to the circumstances and pacify their flesh and not feed their spirit. He taught me to create an environment of expectancy where anyone could come into our worship experience and believe God for the impossible.

There were services in which I got the songs wrong. Then the atmosphere would become heavy, and my husband had to preach harder and didn't get to deliver the message in the way he had received it.

When we did crusades in the auditorium in our early years in London, the first night was salvation, so we would sing songs about the blood to establish heaven's authority for the rest of the night services. Then we would sing songs about the power of God, the blood that cleanses, and miracle songs. The first night was usually the hardest worship night, because we had to discern the audience, read the temperature of the room, and keep the theme of what my husband was going to minister.

The second night was the Holy Spirit night, so this could be people being filled with the Spirit, or the beginning of the healing service. We never ministered to the sick on the first night, as we are establishing our authority in the spirit realm and building the audience's faith for miracles. The second night we would sing songs about a miracle-working God, and all the songs would focus on power, blood, and the greatness of God, once again building the atmosphere by the song choice.

The third night was all about miracles, so every song we sang was about power, blood, and the miracles of God, and we would incorporate the names of God. This is the night that, because of the atmosphere, the audience's faith was built up to where they could expect anything to happen. We could see salvation, people being filled with the Holy Spirit, miracles, healings, and breakthroughs. We prepared the atmosphere for anything.

How did I get it wrong?

Sometimes as I led worship, I realized I had created a salvation atmosphere, so I sang the songs that pertained to people giving their hearts to the Lord, songs about the cross and the blood of Jesus. My husband wanted songs about the blood and the power because of what he was preaching. When it came time to minister the Word, the message had changed, the administration of how he was going to minister changed, so the worship service didn't set the atmosphere for what followed.

But it didn't matter if I got it right or wrong; the next night I was up again leading! However, what this taught me was to trust the Spirit of God within me, and to create an atmosphere for God to move, no matter what the sermon title was.

As we began to record the services in London on videotapes, the challenge was starting the recording from the last song and the moderator's introduction. However, because of copyright laws, we couldn't use a known song; we had to use a song that was unknown. Now I had a new challenge. Without premeditation I would do a simple song spontaneously so that the video person would know when to start recording. Who knew that this would overflow into a worship service being totally spontaneous!

As my husband moved more into teaching about the glory, our worship and administration of the services changed. The sound was very important to building the atmosphere. We fired many worship teams during our conferences if they didn't have the sound that corresponded to what was going on in his spirit. You can imagine how awkward that was. The sound, the building of the atmosphere, the discernment of the movement, and being sensitive to the administration are very important qualities in a worship leader.

> **There was no walkway in front of me, no path laid out for me to follow, and no secure ground in front of me.**

My administration in worship changed many years ago after a dream I had in London. I was standing on a ledge, and there was nothing in front of me. I couldn't see what was a head of me, and I had no compulsion to turn around and go back. However, I knew I was in a worship service, and there was a lot of music around me. As I was standing on the edge, people started leaping over me into nothing. I was quite jealous that they were able to do this. So I asked the Lord to give me the strength or the ability to do that. He said, "Just step out." There was no walkway in front of me, no path laid out for me to follow, and no secure ground in front of me.

As I stepped out, it felt like the movie *Raiders of the Lost Ark*, where Harrison Ford had to go and get the chalice. He came to a ledge, and he had to take a step of faith into nothingness. When he took that first step, a clear walkway came out in front of him, and he walked over to the other side.

This is what happened to me. As I stepped out, there was a clear pathway for me; however, people were still leaping over me and singing songs I had never heard before. I lay down on my back in the middle of nothing, and I said to the Lord, "I don't want this to be a one-time event. Teach me how worship as these do, and teach me to lead others into the unknown."

My growth in the spirit of worship has grown because of my relationship with the Lord. I have learned that He is with me in the difficult times of leading, and He is there speaking in the midst of all worship services. I have learned to open myself up to His voice and obey His leading. My worship team is usually made up of worshippers from different churches in the Dallas, Texas, area. In rehearsal

My Testimony

I always tell them, we will do songs we've practiced, but the opening song will always be spontaneous, meaning it is written out of the atmosphere, and they should be prepared for songs written throughout our worship experience like that. Being able to discern the transition of worship and sound is very important. The songs must match the atmosphere and environment in which God is going to move and display Himself.

Today I have the pleasure of activating worship leaders from around the world to write their songs and find the sound for their house. This is usually done in workshops.

I hope my testimony will encourage you to become a worshipper who sings publicly or privately, and to write your song whether it be personal or for the house where you worship. Give God worship that attracts Him to you. As God inhales your worship (sweet-smelling), He can exhale His glory.

OTHERS PEOPLE'S TESTIMONIES

The following testimonies are from worship leaders I have had the pleasure of working with in our Dallas, Texas, conferences. We have worshiped together and traveled together over the years. They have been able to bring with them a team of worshippers who are open to moving in the presence as I hear and respond to the atmosphere and glory of God. I am so thankful for their gifts and open ears to create an appetite for worship with me.

My name is **Bobby Connors**, and I've known and ministered with Dr. Marina McLean for almost six years. I have been a worship leader for over twenty-five years. I have been fortunate to be on staff for a number of well-known churches in America. To name a few, Word of Faith, Farmers Branch, TX; Calvary Temple, Irving, TX; North Church, Carrollton, TX; High Point, Arlington, TX; New Beginnings, and I currently travel and minister locally.

Ministering with Dr. Marina is different because she truly allows for her worship to infiltrate the heavens where there must be a response. This response brings the glory, which meets people at the point of their need and beyond!

My name is **Becky Mullowney**, and I had the wonderful privilege of leading worship with Marina from 2007–2013, and I am very blessed to still be associated with her ministry. I have been a worship leader for twenty-six years and have served on staff at Providence Church, Destiny Christian Center, and Heritage Church. I have also served as worship leader for various ministries through the years.

When I met Marina, my life changed in a way only God could ordain. We met at a dinner, and we both were thinking we were too busy to be there that night—but God had other plans. I led worship with her the very next evening, and I knew I had truly found a sister in worship. Marina has an amazing voice and is the most gifted person in prophetic song that I have ever met. Her heart for worship and her desire to be in the presence of the Lord takes worshippers to incredible heights in the Spirit; and her spontaneity in prophetic song continually breathes a fresh Rhema word into the worship. There was always an excitement, an expectancy in the worship team because we knew we had absolute freedom to soar however the Spirit led. *Freedom* is the word that keeps coming to mind—freedom for us as worshippers, and freedom for the Spirit to move unhindered. That is an incredible combination, and I will forever be grateful to have experienced it with Marina.

My Worship Journal

Please use these four journal pages to record your personal worship lyrics, poems, prayers, and praises to your Almighty and Radiant God. Be spontaneous and free in expressing your heart and adoration for Him, and listen for His loving response.

_____
_____
_____
_____
_____
_____
_____
_____
_____
_____
_____
_____

_____
_____
_____
_____
_____
_____
_____
_____

Creating a Hunger for His Presence

_____
_____
_____
_____
_____
_____

My Worship Journal

My Worship Journal

Creating a Hunger for His Presence

My Worship Journal

My Prayer as a Worshipper:

Glossary

Sagad Hebrew meaning is from *Strong's Exhaustive Concordance with Hebrew and Greek Lexicon* (Crusade Bible Publishers: Nashville, TN), 1980.

Proskuneo meaning is from *Strong's Exhaustive Concordance with Hebrew and Greek Lexicon* (Crusade Bible Publishers: Nashville, TN), 1980.

Heylel meaning is from *Strong's Exhaustive Concordance with Hebrew and Greek Lexicon* (Crusade Bible Publishers: Nashville, TN), 1980.

Seven redemptive names of God were found on http://www.exit-supportnetwork.com/recovery/names2.htm.

Hebrew words for praise are from *The Basic Pattern of Worship*, found at https://www.umcdiscipleship.org/resources/the-basic-pattern-of-worship.

About the Author

Dr. Marina McLean is known as a worshipper's worshipper, leading worship in different denominations and church conferences for over thirty-five years. Her passion in the last ten years has been leading workshops to activate worship leaders into writing the songs of worship for their spiritual leaders. This has proven to have a big impact on spiritual leaders who have been crying out for songs that testify of the current season of their church.

A sensitivity and intimacy comes when you know how to court the presence of the Lord in any worship experience. Worship leaders are searching for songs that will create an atmosphere in which their spiritual leader can minister the revelation God has entrusted in them for that particular season. Dr. Marina encourages worship leaders to write the songs from the messages that are being released from the pulpits of their churches.

As worshipper, Marina's mandate is to prepare the body of Christ

About the Author

to know how to court the presence of the Lord. She challenges herself to make the believer become a Holy of Holies worshipper and not an outer-court spectator. Finding your identity and purpose is the foundation to destiny and purpose.

As an intercessor and minister, Dr. Marina teaches the sovereign rights of the believer, as we walk in our covenant with the Father. The power is the demonstration of the miracle-working power of God displayed in the circumstances of life.

Dr. Marina has two live worship albums entitled *In The Glory* and *Synchronized,* and *Appetite for Worship* is her latest book.

London-born and of Jamaican descent, Dr. Marina's angelic voice captivates a crowd and ushers in the true presence of God. She was called to ministry as a young child, and her voice was the entrance. Her late parents, Charles and Clarice Headlam, provided the spiritual foundation of the Word and hymns that make her the woman she is today. Growing up, she knew she would travel the world and preach the gospel.

Dr. McLean has a Bachelor of Arts degree in theology and an honorary Doctor of Divinity and Christian Counseling degree from Friends International Christian University.

Dr. Marina has been married for thirty-two years to Dr. Renny McLean. They have three amazing young adult children: Maranatha, Caleb, and Zoe. They reside in Dallas, Texas.

You can stay in touch with Dr. Marina through social media www.facebook.com/marina.mclean.9

Other Worship Products

by
Dr. Marina McLean

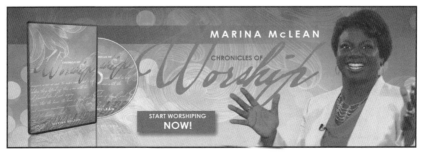

Other Products
by Dr. Marina McLean

Books

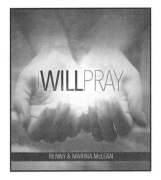

CDs

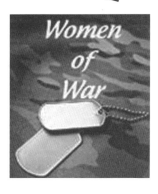

LET'S GET CONNECTED!

Creative Enterprises Studio
1507 Shirley Way, Suite A
Bedford, TX 76022-6737

Facebook.com/CreativeEnterprisesStudio

ACreativeShop@aol.com

CreativeEnterprisesStudio.com